Carbohydrate Counting: Traditional South Asian Food Lists

For Management and Prevention of Diabetes Mellitus

ASHWINI WAGLE, ED.D., M.S., R.D

Contents

Dedication ... i
Acknowledgments ... ii
About the Author ... iii
    Contact Information: ... iv
Introduction ... 1
Maintaining the Balance in Diabetes: Healthy Eating, Physical Activity and Insulin/Medication ... 3
    Healthy Eating in South Asians ... 3
    Physical Activity ... 3
    Stress Management ... 4
    Insulin/Diabetes Medicine ... 5
Carbohydrates (also called Carbs) ... 7
Carbohydrate Counting ... 11
    Food Label ... 13
    How many Carbohydrate Choices am I allowed to eat? ... 13
Sample Meal Plans ... 15
    Planning Your Meals ... 16
    What will I need to get started? ... 17
Proteins ... 18
Fats ... 20
Alcohol ... 22
Food List at a Glance ... 23
Estimate Using a 9-inch Dinner Plate ... 24
Portion Size Estimation ... 25
    My Individual Carbohydrate Goals ... 25
    Measurements and Conversions ... 25
    Tips and Suggestions ... 26
Starches ... 29

Breads....29
Starchy Vegetables....32
Cereals/Grains....33
Pulses/Dals/Beans....37
Fruits....39
Fruits....39
Fruits Juices and Drinks....42
Vegetables....43
Vegetables....43
Sauces....46
Condiments and Sauces....46
Milk and Milk Products....48
Skim Milk/Very Low Fat Milk/Yogurt....48
Low-Fat Milk/Yogurt....49
Whole Milk/Yogurt....49
Whole Milk/Yogurt....49
Dairy-like Foods....50
Combination Foods: Vegetarian....52
Vegetarian Foods....52
Combination Foods: Non-Vegetarian....61
Non-Vegetarian Foods....61
Snack Foods....67
Cakes, Desserts, and Sweets....71
Sugars....74
Beverages, Soda, and Energy/Sports Drinks....75
Proteins....76
Very Lean Protein....77
Lean Protein....78
Medium-Fat Protein....79

High-Fat Protein ... 81
Plant-Based Protein ... 82
Fats ... 84
Unsaturated Fat - Monounsaturated Fat ... 84
Unsaturated Fat - Polyunsaturated Fat ... 85
Saturated Fat ... 86
Free Foods ... 87
Fat-free or Reduced-fat Foods contain < 5g carbs and 20 Calories ... 87
Sugar-free or Low-Carbohydrate Foods contain < 5g carbs and 20 Calories ... 88
Drinks contain < 5g carbs and 20 Calories ... 88
Condiments contain < 5g carbs and 20 Calories ... 89
Free Snacks ... 90
Drinks/Mixes ... 91
Seasonings ... 91
Alcohols ... 92
1500 Calories Sample Menu Plan: North Indian Non-Vegetarian ... 93
1500 Calories Sample Menu Plan: South Indian Non-Vegetarian ... 94
1500 Calories Sample Menu Plan: North Indian Vegetarian ... 95
1500 Calories Sample Menu Plan: South Indian Vegetarian ... 96
1800 Calories Sample Menu Plan: North Indian Non-Vegetarian ... 97
1800 Calories Sample Menu Plan: South Indian Non-Vegetarian ... 99

1800 Calories Sample Menu Plan: North Indian Vegetarian....101
1800 Calories Sample Menu Plan: South Indian Vegetarian....102
2000 Calories Sample Menu Plan: North Indian Non-Vegetarian....103
2000 Calories Sample Menu Plan: South Indian Non-Vegetarian....104
2000 Calories Sample Menu Plan: North Indian Vegetarian....105
2000 Calories Sample Menu Plan: South Indian Vegetarian....106
Carbohydrate Counting Resources....107

Dedication

To my mother Chhaya Wagle and my mother in-law Sangeeta Prabhu, the two giants whose shoulders I stand on.

Acknowledgments

To all my students and colleagues in the field who were a constant source of encouragement for me to develop this tool. To my army of men, my husband, my two sons, my brother, and my father who are the rocks I lean on and my inspiration to always push myself further.

About the Author

Ashwini Wagle, Ed.D, MS, RD is a Professor and the Department Chairperson for the Department of Nutrition, Food Science and Packaging at San Jose State University. She has worked for over twenty years as an educator and also has over ten years of experience as a registered dietitian nutritionist (RDN) in skilled nursing facilities and acute care hospitals in the San Francisco Bay Area. She is involved with several organizations and serves on the committees for the South Asian Heart Center (SAHC) at El Camino Hospital, California Academy of Nutrition and Dietetics (CAND), Silicon Valley District of the California Academy of Nutrition and Dietetics (SVD), and Rise Against Hunger.

Her basic areas of interest and research are food and culture, nutritional implications of traditional health beliefs, dietary practices, and food related behaviors for multicultural, immigrant populations especially South Asians, food insecurity and hunger, and foodservice systems.

She has published several articles in peer reviewed scientific research journals and has presented at national and state conferences.

The Carbohydrate Counting tool was developed to meet the needs of the South Asian population. The contents and the photographs used in the book are an original intellectual product of the author, Dr. Ashwini Wagle.

Contact Information:

Ashwini Wagle, Ed.D, MS, RD
Professor and Department Chairperson,
Department of Nutrition, Food Science and Packaging,
San José State University
Email: ashwini.wagle@sjsu.edu

Introduction

Diabetes is one of the leading causes of morbidity and mortality among South Asians. South Asia is a region comprising countries such as Bangladesh, Bhutan, India, the Maldives, Nepal, Pakistan, and Sri Lanka. Although all ethnic groups are affected by diabetes, the incidence in South Asians living in their home countries and outside the Indian subcontinent is high and is continuing to rise rapidly. Among the South Asian countries, India has the highest prevalence of diabetes in the world.

Diabetes can be managed with:

- Healthy eating (especially carbohydrates)
- Being physically active and managing stress
- Monitoring blood glucose and managing with insulin or diabetes medicine

The standard carbohydrate counting tools available in the United States do not include culturally sensitive ethnic South Asian foods. South Asian dietary practices and habits make up for a complex cuisine that varies from different regions and states throughout the Indian Subcontinent. The cuisine is also influenced by religion, which dictates whether the diet is vegetarian or non-vegetarian. Although there are many similarities in the types of ingredients used and cooking methods, the cuisine can be varied throughout the subcontinent. The staple grain in the cuisine originating from the Northern region and the Western region of the subcontinent is wheat, and the cuisine prevalent in the Eastern and Southern regions of the subcontinent is rice based. The predominant use of pulses and legumes daily makes carbohydrate counting a challenge. This tool will help you get started in planning a healthy South Asian meal of your choice.

Maintaining the Balance in Diabetes:

Healthy Eating, Physical Activity, Stress Management, and Insulin/Medication

Healthy Eating in South Asians

A healthy eating plan includes getting a wide variety of foods each day, watching portion sizes, and choosing foods that are not processed, including:

- Eat three meals a day, and not skipping meals.
- Consuming vegetables, whole grains, fruits, legumes (beans, peas, and lentils), nuts and seeds, low-fat or non-fat dairy products, lean meats, poultry, and fish
- Avoiding processed foods that may contain high amounts of added salt, sugar, or saturated fat/trans fat
- Maintaining healthy weight
- Eating more fiber
- Limiting intake of alcohol
- Knowing blood glucose levels

Physical Activity

Physical activity reduces blood glucose levels. The body uses glucose as a preferred source of fuel, and regular exercises such as walking, hiking, running, swimming, and strength training improve the body's use of insulin and can lower blood glucose levels. Physical activity does not mean sports or workouts at the gym but can include daily activities such as vacuuming, cleaning, gardening, raking leaves, and shoveling snow. Being physically active also helps reduce body fat, lower blood pressure, and protect against heart disease. Recommended physical activity for adults includes at least 150 minutes per week of moderate to vigorous aerobic activity, which averages out to a minimum of 30 minutes of moderate exercise most days of the week. Including resistance exercises in the physical activity regimen, such as weight training and stretches 2-3 times a week, are also beneficial to health.

Stress Management

Stress management is also an important factor in managing Diabetes. Increased stress due to moving away from the homeland or environment (language barrier, difficulty finding a job, family may have become separated when moving) may be detrimental to diabetes management. Good health habits such as healthy eating and regular physical activity can have a protective effect against stress and depression. Yoga and meditation have been known to reduce stress. Stress management classes are also available to help manage stress among South Asians.

Insulin/Diabetes Medicine

Insulin is a hormone made by the pancreas and released into the blood as needed to maintain blood glucose levels. After a meal, the carbohydrates are broken down into glucose, and the blood glucose levels increase. Insulin is produced to help the glucose enter the body's cells to be used for energy.

Type 1 Diabetes: Occurs mostly in young people because the body stops producing insulin leading to an increase in blood glucose levels. Insulin therapy is required for Type 1 Diabetes.

Type 2 Diabetes: Occurs when the body cannot make enough insulin or does not use the insulin it makes properly, leading to an increase in blood glucose levels.

Gestational – occurs during pregnancy.

Blood glucose monitoring is an essential part of daily diabetes management for all people using insulin or oral medications to control their diabetes. Many different types of medications are available to treat diabetes, and diabetes can be treated with diet and exercise, one medication or a combination of medications, medication with insulin, or just insulin alone.

Maintaining the right balance between carbohydrate

intake and insulin regulates blood glucose levels. Insulin doses are measured in units, and matching the insulin to the amount of carbohydrates consumed and adjusting the insulin dosage based on blood glucose levels are important factors. The relationship between units of insulin and grams of carbohydrates is called an insulin-to-carbohydrate ratio and may differ from person to person. Determining when and how much to eat in meals and snacks should be based on the person's lifestyle, medications, and meal-planning goals. Consistency in the amount of carbohydrates eaten at every meal, setting a meal-time maximum for carbohydrates, and matching the insulin taken based on what is being eaten helps control blood glucose levels.

Carbohydrates (also called Carbs)

Carbohydrates are made up of starch, sugar, added sugar, and fiber, and the term "total carbohydrate" on the Nutrition Facts label includes all three types. This is the number that is most important to monitor if you are counting carbohydrates.

Carbohydrates are the body's main source of fuel, and they raise your blood sugar more than any other nutrient. If carbohydrates raise blood glucose, does that mean that, as a diabetic, you should stay away from them? The low-carb diets that are popular today would make you think they are ideal for diabetics. The fact is that current scientific data does not support the long-term use of low-carbohydrate diets, especially in type 2 diabetics.

- The sources for carbohydrates can be varied, and one must choose wisely:
- Select whole grains and less-processed foods such as whole-grain bread, brown rice, whole-grain pasta, and whole wheat rotis over white breads and other refined varieties.
- Consume other types of whole grains, including barley, oats, sorghum, millets, buckwheat, quinoa and bulgur.

- Consume whole fruits with skin instead of fruit juice or fruit snacks.
- Consume a variety of beans, lentils, and other legumes.
- Consume a variety of vegetables.

Carbohydrates from fruits, vegetables, whole grains, and low-fat dairy foods should constitute a healthy diet. Foods from the starch lists, fruits, vegetables, and milk should be the primary sources of carbohydrates for energy, as they also provide vitamins, minerals, and fiber.

The three types of carbohydrates are:

Starch: High starch foods include starchy vegetables like peas, corn, lima beans, cassava, yams, sweet potatoes, and potatoes; legumes (lentils, beans, and peas) like garbanzo beans (chickpeas); kidney beans, pinto beans, black-eyed peas, split peas; pulses; grains like oats, barley, rice, and wheat. Grain-containing foods can be divided further into whole grains and refined grains. Whole-grain foods contain the entire grain (bran, germ, and the endosperm) and contain more nutrients than refined grains.

Sugar: There are two main kinds of sugars: Naturally occurring sugars are found in fruits and milk; Added sugars are sugars used to make desserts and sweets such as cookies, cakes, candies, pies, and ice cream. The total number of sugar (grams) on the Nutrition Facts lable includes both natural and added sugars. However, the added sugar is specified separately.

In the past, people with diabetes were told to 'hold the sugar.' Current scientific literature has found little truth in the notion that sugars raise blood glucose any more than other carbohydrates. The most important factor in controlling blood sugar is the number of carbohydrates eaten in a meal and not the type. What that means is not that you can eat sweets and sugars liberally but that an occasional sweet treat may be okay as long as you make adjustments in the total amount of carbohydrates eaten in that meal.

Fiber: Fiber is the part of plant foods that cannot be digested by the human body and can be found in foods like vegetables, fruits, nuts, beans, and whole grains. Good sources of fiber include legumes like lentils, black beans, kidney beans, chickpeas, split peas, and black-eyed peas; pulses; whole fruits and vegetables, especially those with skin on (apples, pears, peaches, cucumbers, carrots, tomatoes) or those with seeds (berries); whole grains such as whole-wheat pasta, whole-grain cereals, and whole-grain bread; brown rice; nuts (like peanuts, walnuts, or almonds).

Fiber can be found in two types: Soluble Fiber which

dissolves in water and helps reduce glucose and cholesterol levels; Insoluble Fiber helps regulate bowel movements and promotes digestive health. The recommended amounts to eat are 25 to 30 grams of fiber a day, but most Americans eat only about half of the recommended amount. Fiber derived from food is more beneficial than supplements because high-fiber foods contain important vitamins and minerals.

Carbohydrate Counting

Carbohydrate counting, or "carb counting," is a meal-planning technique for managing your blood glucose levels. Carbohydrate counting helps you keep track of amount of carbohydrates you are eating. Carbohydrate counting is not a diet; it is a way of planning your carbohydrate intake to manage your blood glucose levels. It places importance on keeping the carbohydrate content of your meals and snacks consistent from day to day, especially if the person is on diabetes medications. Eating the same amount of carbohydrates for meals and snacks every day, setting meal time maximums for carbohydrates, and matching the insulin plan based on a number of carbohydrates consumed are a few ways to ensure better blood glucose control. The insulin dose can be adjusted based on a number of carbohydrates consumed.

The American Diabetes Association and many health professionals use carbohydrate counting to teach patients how to control their blood glucose. Carbohydrate counting allows for flexibility in meals and snacks and, most importantly, allows one to follow their traditional diet. It allows for better control of blood glucose in people using an insulin pump or taking rapid-acting insulin at meal-times, along with a daily dose of longer-acting insulin to allow for changes in blood glucose. With carbohydrate counting, a person is not bound to consume the same amount of carbohydrates at each meal. Instead, he/she can calculate the amount of carbohydrates eaten and adjust the mealtime rapid-acting insulin dose to match.

One carbohydrate choice is a serving of food that has 15 grams of carbohydrates and comprises of 60-80 Calories. Examples of one carbohydrate choice are a slice of bread or ½ cup of cooked cereal. Look at the food label and measure how much you will be eating. There are two things to locate on the food label; the serving size and the number of grams of carbohydrates per serving. The number of grams of carbohydrates can be used to calculate the number of carbohydrate choices in the amount you are eating by dividing the number of grams of carbohydrate by 15 (1 Carbohydrate Choice); hence read the food label.

Carbohydrate Choices				
	Carbohydrates (grams)	Protein (grams)	Fat (grams)	Calories
Starch/Bread	15	3	trace	80
Vegetable	5	2	-	25
Fruit	15	-	-	60
Milk				
Skim	12	8	0-3	90
Low-fat	12	8	5	120
Whole	12	8	8	150

Food Label

Nutrition Facts

2 servings per container

Serving size	**1 cup (140g)**
Amount per serving	
Calories	**160**
	% Daily Value*
Total Fat 8g	**10%**
Saturated Fat 3g	**15%**
Trans Fat 0g	
Cholesterol 0mg	**0%**
Sodium 60mg	**3%**
Total Carbohydrate 21g	**8%**
Dietary Fiber 3g	**11%**
Total Sugars 15g	
Includes 5g Added Sugars	**10%**
Protein 3g	
Vitamin D 5mcg	**25%**
Calcium 20mg	**2%**
Iron 1mg	**6%**
Potassium 230mg	**4%**

*The % Daily Value tells you how much a nutrient in a serving of food contributes to a daily diet. 2000 calories a day is used for general nutrition advice.

How to Count Carbohydrate Servings

Grams of Carbohydrates	**Carbohydrate Choices**
0-5 grams	free food (do not count)
6-10 grams	½
11-20 grams	1
21-25 grams	1 ½
26-35 grams	2
45 grams	3
60 grams	4
75 grams	5

How many Carbohydrate Choices am I allowed to eat?

You can consult a registered dietitian for an individualized diet plan that fits your needs. Nutrition goals differ depending on the person's goals and lifestyle. Please remember, no one plan fits all. Suggested plans for weight maintenance and weight loss are:

Weight Maintenance:

- Men need approximately 4-5 Carbohydrate choices (60 to 75 grams) at each meal.
- Women generally need about 3-4 Carbohydrate choices (45 to 60 grams) at each meal.
- If you eat snacks, 1 Carbohydrate choice (15 grams) per snack is adequate.

Weight Loss:

- Men need approximately 3-4 Carbohydrate choices (45 to 60 grams) at each meal.
- Women generally need about 2-3 Carbohydrate choices (30 to 45 grams) at each meal.
- If you eat snacks, 1 Carbohydrate choice (15 grams) per snack is adequate.

Sample Meal Plans

The table below shows sample meal plans, by number of servings, for different calorie requirements. (Three servings of vegetables may be consumed to make one carbohydrate choice)

Calories per Day	1200	1500	1600	1800	2000	2200	2500
Carbohydrates Starch (15 grams carb servings)	5	6	7	8	9	10	11
Fruit (15 grams carb servings)	3	3	3	3	4	4	6
Milk (12 grams carb servings)	2	3	3	3	3	3	3
Vegetables (5 grams carb servings)	3	3	3	5	6	6	7
Other Carbohydrates	-	-	-	-	-	-	-
Meat and Meat Substitutes (1 oz per serving)	4	4	6	6	7	8	9

Planning Your Meals

Meal Pattern	No. of Carb choices	No. of Carb choices	No. of Carb choices	No. of Carb choices	No. of Carb choices	No. of Carb choices	No. of Carb choices
	1200 kcal	1500 kcal	1600 kcal	1800 kcal	2000 kcal	2200 kcal	2500 kcal
Breakfast	3	3	3	3	3	4	5
Morning Snack	1	1	1	2	2	2	3
Lunch	3	4	4	4	4	5	5
Afternoon Snack	1	1	1	2	2	2	2
Dinner	2	3	3	3	4	4	5
Evening Snack	1	1	2	2	2	2	2
Total No. of Carb choices	11	13	14	16	17	19	22
Total Grams of Carbs/day	165	195	210	240	255	285	330
Calories from Carbs	660	780	840	960	1,020	1,140	1,320
% of Calories from Carbs	55	52	52	53	51	52	53

What will I need to get started?

You will need a set of measuring cups and spoons plus a food scale. When you are home and able to measure, this comprehensive list will help you to best estimate portion sizes. Food scales can be helpful in counting carbohydrates in home-cooked foods. When you are just beginning to count carbohydrates, you may not be able to accurately estimate a serving size.

Try this: scoop out one serving of rice which should be about 1/3 cup. Now do the same thing using a 1/3 cup measure and see the difference. Once you have been doing it for a few days, you will become better at it and will no longer need the measuring cups.

Proteins

Meat, poultry, fish, eggs, cheese, and plant-based foods such as beans, lentils, peas, and tofu are rich sources of protein. Portion sizes for meats are based on the cooked edible weight of the food after the bones and fat have been removed. Protein foods are divided into four groups (very lean protein, lean protein, medium-fat protein, and high-fat protein) based on the amount of fat they contain. Each serving of meat-based and plant-based protein contains about 7 grams of protein and varies in calories depending on the amount of fat. Plant-based proteins also contain carbohydrates, and therefore calories vary among them, and food labels should be read carefully.

Keep in mind that most adults need only about 6oz of meat or meat alternatives each day. A 3-oz serving of meat is the size of a deck of cards. High-fat proteins are usually high in saturated fat, cholesterol, and calories, so three or fewer choices of high-fat proteins should be consumed per week. Processed meats such as hot dogs, frankfurters, sausages, and deli meats may be high in fat and sodium. Make heart-healthy choices whenever possible and choose lean proteins. Many types of fish, such as salmon, trout, herring, halibut, mackerel, and tuna, are rich sources of omega-3 fats that are known to reduce the risk for heart disease. Healthy eating involves more than just carbohydrate counting.

One protein choice contains 7 grams of protein and is usually:

1 ounce (oz) of meat, poultry, fish, or cheese

1/2 cup of cooked beans, lentils, and peas

Meals may have more than one protein choice. A breakfast meal with one egg, 1 oz cheese, and 1 oz sausage will count for three protein choices. A lunch with 3 oz baked chicken will count for three protein choices. When consuming plant-based protein foods such as vegetarian burgers or meatless patties, one should be aware of "hidden carbohydrates" due to the ingredients used to prepare the foods. Breaded meats, poultry, and fish also contain carbohydrates due to the use of corn flour, wheat, and bread crumbs.

Protein Choices				
	Carbohydrate (grams)	Protein (grams)	Fat (grams)	Calories
Very Lean Protein	-	7	0-1	35
Lean Protein	-	7	3	55
Medium-Fat Protein	-	7	5	75
High-Fat Protein	-	7	8	100
Plant-Based Protein	varies	7	varies	varies

Fats

Fats are divided into three groups: Unsaturated, Saturated, and Trans Fats.

Unsaturated fats are found primarily in plant foods and comprise monounsaturated and polyunsaturated fats (including omega-3 fats).

Monounsaturated fats: Monounsaturated fats can help lower your cholesterol levels and are also known to keep your heart rhythm normal and reduce inflammation. Eating monounsaturated fats also helps regulate insulin and blood sugar levels. Some of the primary sources of monounsaturated fats are liquid oils such as olive, canola, peanut, safflower, and sunflower oils. Almonds, hazelnuts, pecans, pumpkin seeds, and sesame seeds are all good sources of monounsaturated fats.

Polyunsaturated fats: Polyunsaturated fats also help lower bad cholesterol (LDL cholesterol) levels and may also boost good cholesterol (HDL cholesterol) levels, which can reduce the risk of heart disease. A specific kind of polyunsaturated fat, called omega-3 fatty acids, is particularly beneficial to the heart by protecting against high blood pressure and might also reduce the risk of Type 2 diabetes. Good sources of omega-3 fatty acids include fish such as salmon, albacore tuna, halibut, herring, mackerel, trout, and sardines.

Vegetable oils such as canola, corn, soybean, and flaxseed oil are also considered good sources of omega-3 fats. Flaxseeds and walnuts are also rich sources of omega-3 fats.

Saturated fats are primarily found in animal sources and are usually solid at room temperature. Sources of saturated fats include butter, lard, and coconut oil.

Trans fats are considered processed fats as vegetable oils are converted into semi-solid fats and usually comprise partially hydrogenated and hydrogenated fats. Trans fats can be found in vegetable shortenings, margarine, baked goods such as cakes and cookies, candies, snack foods, etc.

All fats are high in calories and should be consumed sparingly. Choose unsaturated fats in comparison to saturated fats or trans fats always. Choose heart-healthy fats from the monounsaturated and polyunsaturated groups more often. It is also recommended to reduce the consumption of fried foods or foods high in fat and sodium content, such as processed snacks. Grilling, baking, or roasting should be the preferred methods of cooking compared to frying.

One fat choice contains 5 grams of fat and 45 calories. Usually, one fat choice equals:

One teaspoon of oil or solid fat

One tablespoon of salad dressing

Alcohol

The use of alcohol should be discussed with the physician and should be used in moderation. The carbohydrate content of alcoholic beverages varies as some beverages contain higher amounts of sugar and carbohydrates. These include sweet wines, sweet vermouth, sweet mixers and wine coolers. Limit beverages with sugar as they may contribute to high blood glucose.

One alcohol equivalent or choice is defined as ½ oz of absolute alcohol and comprises 100 calories.

A “drink” is usually defined as 12 ounces (oz) beer (preferably light beer), a 5-ounce (oz) glass of wine or a 2-ounce (oz) glass of dry sherry or 1.5 ounces (oz) of distilled beverage, such as whiskey, rye, vodka or gin. These beverages contain carbohydrates in addition to the alcohol choice and, therefore may contain additional calories.

It is recommended that women should limit alcohol to 1 serving or less per day and men should limit alcohol to 2 servings per day.

Food List at a Glance

The following chart shows the amount of nutrients in 1 Choice from each list.

Food List	Carbohydrates (grams)	Protein (grams)	Fat (grams)	Calories
Carbohydrates				
Starch/Bread	15	0-3	0-1	80
Non-Starchy Vegetables	5	2	-	25
Fruits	15	-	-	60
Milk: Skim Milk: Low-fat Milk: Whole	12	8	0-3	90
	12	8	5	120
	12	8	8	150
Sweets, Desserts, and Other Carbohydrates	15	varies	varies	varies
Proteins				
Very Lean Protein	-	7	0-1	35
Lean Protein	-	7	3	55
Medium-Fat Protein	-	7	5	75
High-Fat Protein	-	7	8	100
Plant-Based Protein	varies	7	varies	varies
Fats	-	-	5	45
Alcohol	varies	-	-	100

Estimate Using a 9-inch Dinner Plate

Tips:

Make half the plate non-starchy vegetables (10-15 grams carbohydrate or 2/3 to 1 Carb choice).

Make a quarter of the plate protein foods (meat, poultry, fish, eggs)

Make the remaining quarter of the plate starchy foods (30-45 grams of carbohydrate or 2 to 3 carb choices)

Add dairy (1 cup milk, lassi, or 2/3 cup low-fat yogurt) and fruit (1 small) to the meal.

Portion Size Estimation

My Individual Carbohydrate Goals

	Breakfast	Snack	Lunch	Snack	Dinner	Snack
Carbohydrates Starch						
Fruits						
Milk and Milk Products						
Vegetables						
Other Carbohydrates						
Proteins Meat and Meat Substitutes						
Fat						
Free Foods						

Measurements and Conversions

Fluid:

- ½ fluid ounce = 1 tablespoon
- 1 fluid ounce =30 ml = 2 tablespoons
- 1 cup = ½ pint = 240 ml = 8 fluid ounces (oz)
- 2 cups = 1 pint = 480 ml = 16 fluid ounces (oz)
- 1 Katori, 2.25 inches = 100 ml = 3.3 fluid ounces (oz)*

- 1 Katori, 3 inches = 150 ml = 5 fluid ounces (oz)*
- 1 Katori, 3.5 inches = 170 ml = 5.7 fluid ounces (oz)*
- 1 Katori, 4 inches = 200 ml = 6.7 fluid ounces (oz)*
- 1 Katori, 4.5 inches = 240 ml = 8 fluid ounces (oz)*
- 2 pints = 1 quart = 960 ml = 32 fluid ounces (oz)
- 4 quarts = 1 gallon
- 1 quart = 1.0 liter
- 1 teaspoon fluid = 5 ml or 1/6 fluid ounces (oz)
- 1 tablespoon fluid = 15 ml = ½ fluid ounce (oz)

*Katori: A bowl made out of metal (steel, brass, copper, silver) traditionally used as tableware in South Asia.

Dry Measures

- 1 ounce =30 grams
- ½ ounce= 15 grams = 1 tablespoon
- 1 teaspoon = approximately 5 grams
- 1 tablespoon = 3 teaspoons = 15 grams = ½ ounce (oz)
- 1 cup = 8 oz = 16 tablespoons
- ½ cup = 4 oz
- 1 kilogram = 2.2 pounds (2.2 lb)
- 1 pound = 454 grams
- To change pounds to kilograms, multiply by 0.45

Tips and Suggestions

- Eat a variety of foods. Try to include five servings of fruits and vegetables, six servings of grains (three whole grains), and three servings of low-fat dairy daily.

- Foods in the protein (including meat, poultry, and fish) and fat groups do not directly affect blood glucose. However, to keep your heart healthy, some healthy fats (like those found in nuts, seeds, and fish) can be helpful and should be used.
- Foods such as meat, poultry, and fish do not contain carbohydrates, but if they are prepared with sauces, vegetables, or bread, they may contain carbohydrates.
- Substitute brown rice for white rice. Generally, people with diabetes are told to avoid rice altogether. This is a misconception. You can eat rice in reasonable quantities as long as the total carbohydrate for that meal does not exceed your limit.
- Instead of eating only rice, try other grains such as cracked wheat, barley, and quinoa (available in most stores and very high in protein). Use them like you would use rice in pulao etc.
- Avoid starchy vegetables. When using potatoes, yams, or other starchy vegetables, always remember to cut down on the amount of rice/roti eaten at that meal. Better still, select green vegetables in place of starchy ones.
- Use green vegetables freely and prepare them in a small amount of oil.
- Avoid frying as a cooking method; learn to use other methods, such as dry roasting, baking, etc.
- Try to cook with a minimum amount of oil. Use olive or canola oils as they are high in monounsaturated fats, which are good for your heart. Avoid ghee, butter, and cream in cooking.

- Switch to skim or 1% milk and yogurt. When making desserts like kheer, use 1% milk or evaporated skim milk and use artificial sweeteners. Whole milk and yogurt and products made with them, like paneer, are high in saturated fats, which raise cholesterol in your blood. Try making your own paneer and chenna with low-fat milk.
- Tofu is a good source of high-quality protein, especially for vegetarians. Try using it in place of paneer for making dishes like palak paneer.
- Avoid coconut milk/cream or use less than is called for in the recipe. Coconut milk is high in saturated fat.
- Use 100% whole wheat chapatti flour for making rotis/phulkas. Avoid putting any ghee/oil when making rotis.
- Be choosy when eating out and select steamed, tomato-based sauces over cream sauces; choose grilled, roasted, broiled, baked, and poached over fried foods.
- Restaurants usually serve large portions, so be mindful of portion sizes.

Starches

Each item under the Breads, Starchy Vegetables, Cereals/Grains, Pulses/Dals/Beans list contains approximately **one carbohydrate choice** (15 grams of carbohydrate, 3 grams of protein, 0-1 gram of fat, and a total of 80 Calories). The whole grain products contain approximately 2 grams of fiber per serving. Commonly 1/2 cup of cooked cereal, cooked grains, or cooked pasta and one slice (1 oz) of bread or a bread product is equivalent to one serving.

Breads

One carbohydrate choice per Serving
(Each Serving = 15 g Carbohydrate, 3 g protein, 0-1 gm Fat, 80 Calories)

Food	Amount
Appam (Pancake made of Rice Batter)	1, 8″ diameter
Appe, Paniyaram	2 each
Bagel, Egg	¼ (1 oz)
Biscuit	1, 2.5″ diameter
Bread sticks (Crisp)	2, 4″ long and ½″ thick (⅔ oz)
Bread (White, Wheat, Rye, Wholegrain)	1 slice (1 oz)
Bread, Pumpkin	1 slice (1 oz)
Bread, Raisin unfrosted	1 slice (1 oz)
Bread, Reduced-calorie	2 slices (1½ oz)
Cornbread	1 ¾″ (1½ oz)
Croissant	1 small (1 oz)
Dinner Roll (Pav)	1 small (1 oz)
Dosa, Neer	1, 8″ diameter
Dosa, Plain (Pancake made of Fermented Batter)	1, 8″ diameter
Dosa, Paneer (Pancake stuffed with Paneer)	1, 6″ diameter
Dosa, Rava (Pancake made of Semolina Batter)	1, 6″ diameter
English Muffin	½ (1 oz)
Hamburger/Hot Dog bun	½ (1 oz)
Idli, Plain (Dumplings made of Fermented Batter)	1 small, 3″ round (1½ oz)
Idli, Rava (Dumplings made of Fermented Semolina Batter)	2 mini, 1 ½ "round, (1½ oz)
Khakara, Readymade (Crisp Seasoned Bread)	1, 10″ diameter
Kulcha, Plain, Garlic or Onion, Leavened Flat bread*	1/2, 6′ diameter
Muffin*	1 small
Muffin, Oat Bran*	1 small
Naan, Tandoori (Leavened Flat bread made in a Clay Oven)	¼, 8″ x 2″
Naan, Mini Stonefire Brand	½ each

Food	Amount
Pancake	1, 4″ diameter x ¼″ thick
Paratha Paneer (Paneer Stuffed Bread)*	½, 6″ diameter
Paratha Plain or Thepla (Pan Fried Bread)*	¾, 6″ diameter
Paratha Aloo (Potato Stuffed Bread)*	¾, 6″ diameter
Paratha, Green Leafy Vegetables (Fenugreek, Spinach, Radish Greens Stuffed Bread)*	1, 6″ diameter
Paratha Roghani*	½, 6″ diameter
Pita Bread	½, 6″ diameter
Puran Poli, Holige, Vermi, Lanchipoli, Bobbatlu (Sweet Lentil Stuffed Bread)	½, 6″ diameter
Puri* (Fried Bread)	2, 4″ diameter
Puri, Bhatura (Fried Leavened Bread)*	½, 6″ diameter
Puri, Methi (Fried Unleavened Bread with Fenugreek)*	2, 4″ diameter
Roti, Chapati (Unleavened Flat Bread)	1, 6″ diameter
Roti, Phulka (Unleavened Flat Bread)	1, 6″ diameter
Roti (Bajra, Corn/Makai, Jowar, Multi-grain)	¾, 6″ diameter
Roti, Khakara (Crisp Seasoned Bread)	1, 10″ diameter
Roti, Multigrain/Missi	¾″, 6″ diameter
Roti, Roomali*	½, 12″ diameter
Stuffing, Bread	⅓ cup
Taco shell or Tostada shell	2 crisp shells, 5″ across
Tortilla: Corn or Flour Flour	 1, 6″ across ⅓, 10″ across
Uttapam (Vegetable or Plain)	1, 4″ diameter
Waffle, Buttermilk	1, 4″ square or diameter
Waffle	1, 4″ square or diameter

* These items also contain 5 grams of fat and are counted as 1 starch and 1 fat choice.

Starchy Vegetables

One carbohydrate choice per Serving
(Each Serving = 15 g Carbohydrate, 3 g protein, 0-1 gm Fat, 80 Calories)

Food	Amount
Breadfruit	¼ cup
Cassava, Dasheen	⅓ cup
Corn on the Cob (Bhutta)	1, 6″ (5 oz)
Corn (Makai)	½ cup
Hominy, Canned	¾ cup
Malanga	⅓ cup
Mixed Veg (Corn, Peas)	½ cup
Parsnips (Chukander)	½ cup
Peas, Green (Matar, Vatana)	½ cup
Plantain, Green (Katcha Kela)	⅓ cup
Plantain, Ripe (Kela)	⅓ cup
Potato Sabji*(Aloo Sabzi)	½ cup
Potato, Boiled or Baked (Aloo)	½ cup or 1 small (3 oz)
Potatoes, Fried French Fries*	10 (2 oz)
Potatoes, Hashbrowns*	⅓ cup
Potatoes, Mashed	½ cup
Pumpkin Puree, Canned (No Sugar Added)	1 cup
Pumpkin, Cooked (Kaddu)	½ cup
Pumpkin Sabzi*	½ cup
Succotash	½ cup
Sweet Potatoes (Shakarkand, Ratale)	½ cup
Shakarkand Sabzi*	½ cup
Winter Squash (Acorn or Butternut)	1 cup
Squash Sabzi*	½ cup
Yams (Jimikand, Suran)	½ cup

* These items also contain 5 grams of fat and are counted as 1 starch and 1 fat choice.

Cereals/Grains

One carbohydrate choice per Serving
(Each Serving = 15 g Carbohydrate, 3 g protein, 0-1 gm Fat, 80 Calories)

Food	Amount
Amaranth Cooked (Rajgira)	⅓ cup
Amaranth Raw (Rajgira)	1 2/3 Tbsp (20 g)
Amaranth Flour (Rajgire ka Atta)	2 Tbsp
Barley, Cooked (Jau, Jav)	½ cup
Barley, Raw (Jau, Jav)	2 ¼ Tbsp (20 g)
Bran Cereals	½ cup
Buckwheat, Cooked (Kuttu)	½ cup
Buckwheat, Raw (Kuttu)	1 ¾ Tbsp (20 g)
Buckwheat Groats, Cooked (Sabut Kuttu)	½ cup
Buckwheat Groats, Raw (Sabut Kuttu)	2 ¼ Tbsp (25 g)
Buckwheat Flour (Kuttu ka Atta)	3 Tbsp
Bulgur, Cooked	½ cup
Bulgur, Raw	2 Tbsp (20 g)
Cereals -Bran -Oatmeal, Cooked -Puffed -Shredded wheat, plain -Ready to eat, unsweetened -Sugar-frosted	 ½ cup ½ cup 1½ cups ½ cup ¾ cup ½ cup
Cream of Wheat or Rice, Cooked	½ cup
Cream of Wheat or Rice, Raw	1 ¾ Tbsp (20 g)
Corn, Cooked/Boiled (Makai)	½ cup
Corn, Roasted (Lime Juice and Spices)	½ cup

Food	Amount
Corn, Raw (Makai)	⅓ cup (60 g)
Cornmeal, Cooked	⅓ cup
Cornmeal, Uncooked	2 Tbsp (20 g)
Couscous, Cooked	⅓ cup
Couscous, Raw	2 Tbsp (20 g)
Granola, Regular or Low Fat	¼ cup
Grape-Nuts®	¼ cup
Grits, Cooked	½ cup
Kasha	½ cup
Maize, Cooked	½ cup
Maize, Raw	2 Tbsp (20 g)
Masa, Uncooked	2 Tbsp
Matzo Balls	2 (1 oz each)
Matzo Ball Soup	1 cup
Matzo Meal, Uncooked	2 Tbsp
Millet, Barnyard Cooked (Samo, Samvat, Varai)	⅓ cup
Millet, Barnyard Raw (Samo, Samvat, Varai)	1 ¾ Tbsp (20 g)
Millet, Finger Cooked (Ragi/Nachni)	⅓ cup
Millet, Finger Raw (Ragi/Nachni)	1 ¾ Tbsp (20 g)
Millet, Foxtail Cooked (Kangni, Navane, Rala)	⅓ cup
Millet, Foxtail Raw (Kangni, Navane, Rala)	1 ¾ Tbsp (20 g)
Millet, Little Cooked (Kutki, Samai)	⅓ cup
Millet, Little Raw (Kutki, Samai)	1 ¾ Tbsp (20 g)
Millet, Pearl Cooked (Bajra)	⅓ cup
Millet, Pearl Raw (Bajra)	1 ¾ Tbsp (20 g)
Muesli	¼ cup
Oats, Cooked (Jai, Javie, Jawie)	½ cup
Oats, Raw Whole Grain (Jai, Javie, Jawie)	5 Tbsp (25 g)

Food	Amount
Oats, Rolled Oats Cooked (Jai, Javie, Jawie)	½ cup
Oats, Rolled Raw (Jai, Javie, Jawie)	5 Tbsp (25 g)
Pasta Cooked	⅓ cup
Pasta Dry Uncooked	⅓ cup (25 g)
Polenta, Cooked	⅓ cup
Polenta, Raw	1 ⅓ Tbsp (20 g)
Quinoa, Cooked	⅓ cup
Quinoa, Raw	2 ¼ Tbsp (25 g)
Rice, Brown Cooked (Chawal, Bhat)	⅓ cup
Rice, Brown Raw	1 ½ Tbsp (20 g)
Rice, Curd or Yogurt (Thayir Saadam, Dahi Chawal)	½ cup
Rice Flakes, Cooked (Poha)	½ cup
Rice Flakes, Dry (Poha)	¼ cup (20 g)
Rice, Puffed (Murmura, Churmure)	1 ¼ cup
Rice, Vermicelli Cooked (Seviyan)	⅓ cup
Rice, Vermicelli Raw (Seviyan)	1 ½ Tbsp (20 g)
Rice, White Cooked (Chawal, Bhat)	⅓ cup
Rice, White Raw (Chawal, Bhat)	1 ½ Tbsp (20 g)
Sorghum, Cooked (Jowar)	⅓ cup
Sorghum, Raw (Jowar)	1 ¾ Tbsp (20 g)
Tapioca, Cooked (Sabudana)	⅓ cup
Tapioca, Uncooked (Sabudana)	2 Tbsp (20 g)
Wheat, Cracked, Cooked (Dalia)	1/8 cup
Wheat, Cracked (Dalia)	2 Tbsp (20 g)
Wheat Germ, Dry	6 ¼ Tbsp (35 g)
Wheat, Semolina (Sooji/Rava)	¼ cup (20 g)
Wheat, Shredded	½ cup (20 g)

Food	Amount
Wheat, Sprouted	⅓ cup (40 g)
Wheat, Vermicelli Cooked (Seviyan)	⅓ cup
Wheat, Vermicelli Raw (Seviyan)	2 ¾ Tbsp (20 g)
Whole Wheat Flour (Gehun ka Atta)	2 ½ Tbsp (20 g)
All-Purpose Flour (Maida)	2 ¾ Tbsp (20 g)
Wild Rice, Cooked	½ cup
Wild Rice, Raw	1 ¾ Tbsp (20 g)

Pulses/Dals/Beans

1 Carbohydrate choice and 1 Very Lean Protein choice

(Each Serving = 15 g Carbohydrate, 7 g protein, 0-3gm Fat, 125 Calories)

Food	Amount
Baked Beans	⅓ cup
Bengal Gram, Cooked (Chole, Kabuli Chana, Chickpeas, Garbanzo)	½ cup
Bengal Gram, Raw (Chole, Kabuli Chana, Chickpeas, Garbanzo)	2 Tbsp (25 g)
Bengal Gram Split, Cooked (Chana Dal)	½ cup
Bengal Gram Split, Raw (Chana Dal)	2 Tbsp (25 g)
Bengal Gram or Chick Pea Flour (Besan)	⅓ cup
Black Eyed Peas, Cooked (Chavli)	½ cup
Black Eyed Peas, Raw (Chavli)	2 Tbsp (25 g)
Black Gram, Split Polished Cooked (Urad Dal)	½ cup
Black Gram, Polished Raw (Urad Dal)	2 Tbsp (25 g)
Black Gram, Split Cooked (Sabut Urad Dal)	½ cup
Black Gram, Split Raw (Sabut Urad Dal)	2 Tbsp (25 g)
Black Gram, Whole Cooked (Urad)	½ cup
Black Gram, Whole Raw (Urad Dal)	2 Tbsp (25 g)
Field Beans, Split Cooked (Kadve Val)	½ cup
Field Beans, Split Raw (Kadve Val)	2 Tbsp (25 g)
Field Beans, Whole Cooked (Kadve Val)	½ cup
Field Beans, Whole Raw (Kadve Val)	2 Tbsp (25 g)
Green Gram, Cooked (Moong Dal)	½ cup
Green Gram, Raw (Moong Dal)	2 Tbsp (25 g)
Green Gram Whole, Cooked (Moong Beans)	½ cup
Green Gram Whole, Raw (Moong Beans)	2 Tbsp (25 g)

Food	Amount
Green Gram Whole, Sprouted (Moong Beans)	1 ½ cup
Green Gram Whole (Moong Missal/Usal)	½ cup
Green Gram, Sprouted (Moong Salad with Potatoes)	1 cup
Horse Gram, Cooked (Kulith)	½ cup
Horse Gram, Raw (Kulith)	2 Tbsp (25 g)
Kidney Beans, Cooked (Rajma)	½ cup
Kidney Bean, Raw (Rajma)	2 Tbsp (25 g)
Lentils, Brown/Green/Yellow, Split Cooked (Masoor Dal)	½ cup
Lentils, Brown/Green/Yellow, Split Raw (Masoor Dal)	2 Tbsp (25 g)
Lentils, Brown/Green/Yellow, Whole Cooked (Masoor Dal)	½ cup
Lentils, Brown/Green/Yellow, Whole Raw (Masoor Dal)	2 Tbsp (25 g)
Lima Beans, Cooked (Spem, Papdi, Fafda Papdi)	⅔ cup
Moth Beans, Cooked (Matki)	½ cup
Moth Beans, Raw (Matki)	2 Tbsp (25 g)
Moth Beans (Matki) Ussal	½ cup
Peas, Cooked (Vatana)	½ cup
Peas, Dry Raw (Vatana)	2 Tbsp (25 g)
Red Gram, Cooked (Toor/Arhar Dal)	½ cup
Red Gram, Raw (Toor/Arhar Dal)	2 Tbsp (25 g)
Refried Beans, Canned	½ cup
Sambhar	½ cup
Split Peas, Cooked (Matar)	½ cup
Split Peas, Raw (Matar)	2 Tbsp (25 g)
Soybean Cooked (Bhatma)	⅔ cup
Soybean Raw (Bhatma)	4 Tbsp (50 g)
Soy Flour	3 Tbsp

Fruits

Each item on the fruit list contains approximately one carbohydrate choice
(15 grams of carbohydrate and a total of 60 Calories). Fruits have about 2 grams of fiber per serving.

Food	Amount
Fresh or Canned Fruits (Unsweetened)	½ cup
Dried Fruit	¼ cup
Fruit Juice	½ cup

Fruits

One carbohydrate choice per Serving
(Each Serving = 15 g Carbohydrate, 0 g protein, 0 gm Fat, 60 Calories)

Food	Amount
Apple, Raw (Seb, Safarchand)	1 small, 2" across
Apple, Dried	4 rings
Applesauce (Unsweetened)	½ cup
Apricots, Canned (Jardalu)	½ cup
Apricots, Dried	8 halves
Apricots, Raw	4 whole, medium
Banana (Kela)	1 small (4 oz) or ½ medium
Blackberries, Dried	1½ Tbsp
Blackberries, Raw (Kale Shahtut)	¾ cup
Blueberries, Dried	1 ½ Tbsp
Blueberries, Raw	¾ cup

Food	Amount
Cantaloupe (Kharbuja)	⅓ melon, 5" across
Cantaloupe, Cubes	1 cup
Cherries, Canned	½ cup
Cherries, Raw	12 large
Clementine	2 each
Cranberries, Dried	2 Tbsp
Cranberries, Raw	½ cup
Custard Apple (Seetaphal)	1 medium
Dates (Khajur)	2 ½ medium (deglet noor) or 1 large (mejdool)
Dried Fruits	1/8 cup or 2Tbsp
Figs, Dried (Anjeer)	3 small
Figs, Raw	1½ large or 2 medium
Fruit Cocktail, Canned	½ cup
Grapefruit Segments (Chakotara)	¾ cup
Grapefruit	½ large (11 oz)
Grapes (Angoor, Draksha)	17 (3 oz), small
Guava (Amrud, Peru)	2 small or 1 large

Food	Amount
Honeydew Melon Cubes (Kharbuja)	1 cup
Honeydew Melon (Kharbuja)	1 slice (10 oz)
Jackfruit, Sliced or Pieces (Kathal, Phanas)	½ cup
Jambu/Jamun	6
Kiwi (Kiwiphal)	1
Lemon (Nimbu)	3 small or 1 large
Lichi or Lychees	10
Loquat	4 or ¾ cup cubed
Mandarin Oranges, Canned (Santra, Narangi)	¾ cup
Mix Fruit, Dried	2 Tbsp
Mango (Aam, Amba)	½ small (½ cup)
Nectarine	1 small
Orange (Santra, Narangi)	1 small
Papaya Raw Cubes	1 cup
Passion Fruit	½ medium
Peach, Raw (Aadu, Shaphatalu)	1 medium (¾ cup)
Peaches/Pears, Canned	½ cup or 2 halves
Pear Raw (Nashpati)	½ large
Pineapple, Canned (Ananas)	½ cup
Pineapple, Raw (Ananas)	¾ cup
Plums, Canned	½ cup
Plums, Dried	3
Plums, Raw (Alubukhara, Ber)	2 small
Pomegranate (Anar)	½ cup
Prunes, Dried (Sukha Alubukhara)	3
Raisins (Munaka, Kishmish)	2 Tbsp
Raspberries, Raw	1 cup
Raspberries, Dried	2 Tbsp
Sapota (Chikoo)	1 medium
Strawberries Raw	1¼ cup, whole
Tangerine, Raw (Santra, Narangi)	2 small
Watermelon, Cubed (Tarbooz)	1¼ cup

Fruit Juices, and Drinks

One carbohydrate choice per Serving

(Each Serving = 15 g Carbohydrate, 0 g protein, 0 gm Fat, 60 Calories)

Food	Amount
Apple Juice/Cider	½ cup
Apricot Juice	½ cup
Carrot Juice	½ cup
Coconut Water	1 cup
Cranberry Juice Cocktail	⅓ cup
Cranberry Juice Cocktail, Reduced-Calorie	1 cup
Energy Drink	½ cup (4 oz)
Fruit Drink or Lemonade	½ cup (4 oz)
Fruit Juice Bar, Frozen (100% Fruit)	1 (3 oz)
Fruit Juice Blends, 100% Juice	⅓ cup
Grapefruit Juice	½ cup
Grape Juice	⅓ cup
Guava Juice	½ cup
Mango Juice	⅓ cup
Orange Juice	½ cup
Papaya Juice	½ cup
Pineapple Juice	½ cup
Pomegranate Juice	½ cup
Prune Juice	⅓ cup
Soft Drink, Soda	5 oz
Sports Drink	1 cup (8oz)
Strawberry Juice	½ cup
Tomato Juice	½ cup
V8 Juice	½ cup

Vegetables

Each vegetable on this list contains approximately 5 grams of carbohydrates, 2 grams of protein, 0 grams of fat, and a total of 25 Calories. Vegetables contain 2-3 grams of dietary fiber.

Food	Amount
Cooked Vegetables	½ cup
Raw Vegetables	1 cup
Vegetable Juice	½ cup

Vegetables

Count as One carbohydrate choice if serving size more than 15 g *(Each Serving = 5 g Carbohydrate, 2 g protein, 0 gm Fat, 25 Calories)*

Food	Amount
Amaranth Leaves (Chauli ki Sabzi, Lal Maath)	½ cup cooked
Artichokes Cooked (Vajrangee, Hathi Chaak)	1 medium
Asparagus (Shatavar, Sootmooli)	½ cup cooked
Avocado, Raw (Makhanphal)	1/3 medium
Beans Broad (Papadi)	½ cup cooked
Beans Cluster (Gawar)	½ cup cooked
Beans French (Farash Beans, Fansi)	½ cup cooked
Beans Green (Sem Phalli)	½ cup cooked
Bean Sprouts (Ankurit Phaliyan)	1 cup raw
Beetroot (Chukander)	½ cup cooked
Bell Pepper (Capsicum, Simla Mirch)	½ cup cooked
Bok Choy (Chinese Cabbage)	½ cup cooked

Food	Amount
Broccoli (Hari Phool Gobi)	½ cup cooked
Brussels Sprouts (Choti Band Gobi)	½ cup cooked
Cabbage (Band Patta Gobi)	½ cup cooked
Carrots (Gajar)	½ cup cooked
Cauliflower (Phool Gobi)	½ cup cooked
Celery stalk (Aajmoda)	½ cup cooked
Colacasia Leaves Curry (Arbi Patta, Alu)	½ cup cooked
Corn, White (Kanas, Makka)	½ cup cooked
Corn, Yellow (Kanas, Makka)	½ cup cooked
Cucumber (Kakadi, Kheera)	½ cup cooked
Dill Leaves (Shepu)	½ cup cooked
Drumstick (Shevgyacha Shenga, Sahjan ki Phalli)	½ cup cooked
Drumstick leaves (Sahjan)	½ cup cooked
Egg Plant (Brinjal, Baingan)	½ cup cooked
Fenugreek Leaves (Methi)	½ cup cooked
Gourd Ash, Winter Melon (Petha)	½ cup cooked
Gourd Bitter, Bitter Melon (Karela)	½ cup cooked
Gourd Bottle (Dudhi, Ghiya, Lauki)	½ cup cooked

Food	Amount
Gourd Ivy, Gourd Little (Tindora, Tendli)	½ cup cooked
Gourd, Indian Round (Tinda)	½ cup cooked
Gourd Pointed (Paraval)	½ cup cooked
Gourd Ridge (Shirale, Turiya, Turai)	½ cup cooked
Gourd Snake (Chichinda)	½ cup cooked
Greens (Collard, Kale, Swiss Chard, Turnip)	½ cup cooked
Kohlrabi	½ cup cooked
Lotus Stem or Root (Kamal Kakdi)	½ cup cooked
Mixed Vegetables	½ cup cooked
Mushrooms (Kumbhee)	½ cup cooked
Mustard Greens (Sarson ka Saag)	½ cup cooked
Okra (Ladies Finger, Bhindi)	½ cup cooked
Onions (Pyaz/Kanda)	½ cup cooked
Peas (Matar, Vatana)	½ cup cooked
Plantain, Green (Katcha Kela)	½ cup cooked
Potato (Aloo)	½ cup cooked
Pumpkin (Kaddu)	½ cup cooked
Radish (Mooli)	½ cup cooked
Snap Peas (Matar Phalli)	½ cup cooked
Sorrel Leaves (Gongura, Ambaadi)	½ cup cooked
Spinach (Palak)	½ cup cooked
Squash Chayote	1 cup cooked
Squash (Winter, Acorn, Hubbard)	½ cup cooked
Sweet Potatoes (Shakarkand, Ratale)	½ cup cooked
Taro, Colocasia (Arbi, Alu)	½ cup cooked
Tomato (Tamatar)	½ cup cooked
Turnip (Shalgam, Navalkhol)	½ cup cooked
Water Chestnuts (Singhada)	½ cup cooked
Yam (Suran, Jimikand)	½ cup cooked
Zucchini (Dodki, Tori)	½ cup cooked

Sauces

Food	Amount
Pasta/Spaghetti sauce	½ cup
Tomato Puree	¼ cup
Tomato Sauce	½ cup

Condiments and Sauces

Food	Amount	Composition
Barbecue Sauce	3 Tbsp	1 Carbohydrate
Chili Sauce, Sweet, Tomato-Type	¼ cup	1 Carbohydrate
Coconut Chutney	2 Tbsp	½ Carbohydrate, 1 Fat
Carrot-Turnip (Gajar-Shalgam) Achar, Pickle	¼ cup	½ Carbohydrate, 2 Fat
Cranberry Sauce, Jellied	¼ cup	1 ½ Carbohydrate
Curry Sauce	1 oz	1 Carbohydrate, 1 Fat
Gooseberry Pickle Sweet, Amla Morabba	1 Tbsp	1 Carbohydrate
Gravy, Canned or Bottled	½ cup	½ Carbohydrate, ½ Fat
Green Mango Pickle Spicy, Achar	2 Tbsp	1 Fat
Hoisin Sauce	1 Tbsp	½ Carbohydrate
Lemon Pickle, Spicy	1 Tbsp	1 Fat
Lemon Pickle, Sweet	1 Tbsp	1 Carbohydrate, 1 Fat
Mango Pickle Sweet, Chunda	1 Tbsp	1 Carbohydrate
Mango Pickle Sweet, Morabba	1 Tbsp	1 Carbohydrate
Peanut Chutney with Yogurt	½ cup	1 Carbohydrate, 1 Fat
Peri Peri Sauce	2 Tbsp	½ Fat

Food	Amount	Composition
Plum Sauce	1 Tbsp	½ Carbohydrate
Salad Dressing, Fat-Free, Cream-Based	3 Tbsp	1 Carbohydrate
Sweet and Sour Sauce	3 Tbsp	1 Carbohydrate
Tamarind Chutney	2 Tbsp	1 Carbohydrate
Tandoori Marinade	2 Tbsp	½ Carbohydrate
Tomato Chutney	2 Tbsp	1 Carbohydrate
Mixed Vegetable Pickle (Pachranga)	¼ cup	½ Carbohydrate, 2 Fat

Milk and Milk Products

Each serving of milk and milk products on this list contains approximately 12 grams of carbohydrates and 8 grams of protein. The total number of Calories will vary on the amount of fat in the kind of milk chosen. The list is divided into skim/very low-fat milk/yogurt, low-fat milk/yogurt, whole milk/yogurt, and dairy-like foods.

	Carbohydrate (g)	Protein (g)	Fat (g)	Calories
Skim	12	8	trace	90
Low-fat	12	8	5	120
Whole	12	8	8	150

Skim Milk/Very Low-Fat Milk/Yogurt

(Each Serving = 12 g Carbohydrate, 8 g protein, 0-3 g Fat, 90 Calories)

Food	Amount
Buttermilk Non-Fat or Low-Fat 1%	1 cup
Chocolate Milk Low-Fat	½ cup
Dry Milk Powder Non-Fat	⅓ cup
Evaporated Skim Milk	½ cup
Masala Chai made with 1% milk	1 cup
Milk 1%	1 cup
Milk Fat-Free	1 cup
Plain Yogurt Non-Fat	2/3 cup
Yogurt Fruit Flavor, Artificial Sweetener	1 cup

Low-Fat Milk/Yogurt

(Each Serving = 12 g Carbohydrate, 8 g protein, 5 g Fat, 120 Calories)

Food	Amount
Buttermilk Low-Fat 2%	1 cup
Kefir	1 cup
Lassi Low-Fat, Artificial Sweetener	1 cup
Milk 2%	1 cup
Plain Yogurt Low-Fat	2/3 cup

Whole Milk/Yogurt

(Each Serving = 12 g Carbohydrate, 8 g protein, 8 gm Fat, 150 Calories)

Food	Amount
Buttermilk Whole	1 cup
Evaporated Whole Milk	½ cup
Goat's Milk	1 cup
Lassi, Artificial Sweetener	1 cup
Plain Yogurt Regular	2/3 cup
Sweet Acidophilus Milk	1 cup
Whole Milk	1 cup

Whole Milk/Yogurt

(Each Serving = 1 gm Carbohydrate, 7 g protein, 8 g Fat, 100 Calories)

Food	Amount	Composition
Paneer	1/4 cup (1 ½ oz)	1 Protein, 1 ½ Fat, 100 Calories

Dairy-like Foods

15g Carbohydrate (1 Carbohydrate choice), 7g Protein (1 Protein choice) and 5g Fat (1 Fat choice)

Food	Amount	Composition
Almond Milk	1 cup	½ Carbohydrate, 1 Fat, 60 Calories
Almond Milk, Chocolate	1 cup	1 ½ Carbohydrate, 1 Fat, 120 Calories
Almond Milk, Vanilla	1 cup	1 Carbohydrate, 1 Fat, 90 Calories
Chocolate milk		
Fat-free	1 cup	2 Carbohydrate, 1 Protein, 140 Calories
Low-fat 1%	1 cup	1 ½ Carbohydrate, 1 Protein, ½ Fat, 160 Calories
Whole	1 cup	1 ½ Carbohydrate, 1 Protein, 1 ½ Fat, 208 Calories
Hot Chocolate Mix	1 envelope, 2Tbsp	1 Carbohydrate
Eggnog		
Fat-free	½ cup	1 ½ Carbohydrate, ½ Protein, 100 Calories
Low-fat 1%	½ cup	1 ½ Carbohydrate, ½ Protein, ½ Fat, 130 Calories 1
Low-fat 2%	½ cup	½ Carbohydrate, 1 Protein, ½ Fat, 150 Calories
Whole milk	½ cup	1 ½ Carbohydrate, ½ Protein, 2 ½ Fat, 230 Calories
Lassi		
Mango Lassi		
Rose Lassi	1 cup	2 Carbohydrate, 1 Protein, 1 Fat, 185 Calories
Sweet	1 cup	2 ½ Carbohydrate, 1 Protein, 1 Fat, 210 Calories
Lassi	1 cup	1 ½ Carbohydrate, 1 Protein, ½ Fat, 130 Calories
Rice milk		
Vanilla Flavored	1 cup	2 Carbohydrate, ½ Fat, 150 Calories
Regular, Plain	1 cup	1 ½ Carbohydrate, ½ Fat, 115 Calories
Saffron Milk with Nuts, Masala Dudh	1 cup	1 ½ Carbohydrate, 1 Protein, 1 Fat, 180 Calories
Smoothies, Fruit	1 cup	2 Carbohydrate, 1 Protein, ½ Fat, 160 Calories
Soy milk		
Light, Plain	1 cup	½ Carbohydrate, 1 Protein, 70 Calories
Regular, Plain	1 cup	½ Carbohydrate, 1 Protein, 1 Fat, 100 Calories
Vanilla Flavored	1 cup	1 Carbohydrate, 1 Protein, 1 Fat, 130 Calories
Thandai	1 cup	1 ½ Carbohydrate, 1 ½ Protein, 1 ½ Fat, 245 Calories

Food	Amount	Composition
Yogurt, Greek		
Nonfat Plain	2/3 cup (5.3oz)	2 Protein, 90 Calories
Low-fat Plain	2/3 cup (5.3oz)	½ Carbohydrate, 2 Protein, 1 Fat, 110 Calories
Whole Plain	2/3 cup (5.3oz)	½ Carbohydrate, 2 Proteins, 2 Fat, 150 Calories
Nonfat Vanilla or Fruit or Chocolate	2/3 cup (5.3oz)	1 Carbohydrate, 2 Proteins, 120 Calories
Low-fat vanila or Fruit	2/3 cup (5.3oz)	1 Carbohydrate, 2 Proteins, 1 Fat, 145-150 Calories
Whole Vanilla or Fruit	2/3 cup (5.3oz)	1 Carbohydrate, 2 Proteins, 2 Fat, 180 Calories
Yogurt		
Nonfat with Fruit or Juice Blends	2/3 cup (6oz)	2 Carbohydrate, 1 Protein, 160 Calories
Low-fat with Fruit or Juice Blends	2/3 cup (6oz)	2 Carbohydrate, 1 Protein, 1 Fat, 175 Calories
Low Carbohydrate	2/3 cup (6oz)	2 Protein, ½ Fat, 90 Calories

Combination Foods: Vegetarian

The Combination Foods list contains foods commonly consumed by the South Asian population. The amount of calories from carbohydrates and fat varies depending on the food consumed.

Vegetarian Foods

15g Carbohydrate (1 Carbohydrate choice), 7g Protein (1 Protein choice), and 5g Fat (1 Fat choice)

Food	Amount	Composition
Aloo Gobi (Potatoes and Cauliflower)	½ cup	1 Carbohydrate, 1 Fat
Aloo Matar (Potatoes and Peas)	½ cup	1 Carbohydrate, 1 Fat
Aloo Methi Sabzi (Potatoes and Fenugreek)	½ cup	1 Carbohydrate, 1 Fat
Aloo Palak Sabzi (Potatoes and Spinach)	¾ cup	1 Carbohydrate, 1 Fat
Aloo Puri	½ cup Sabzi + 2, 4″ diameter Puris	2 Carbohydrate, 3 Fat
Appam with Coconut Milk	1, 8″ diameter	1 Carbohydrate, 2 Fat
Appe with Coconut Chutney	2 each + 2 tbsp Chutney	1 ½ Carbohydrate, 2 Fat
Aviyal	½ cup	1 Carbohydrate, 2 Fat
Batata Poha or Savory Rice Flakes with Potatoes	1 cup	1 ½ Carbohydrate, 1 Fat
Batata Vada, Fried	1 piece (30 g)	1 ½ Carbohydrate, 2 Fat
Batata Vada and Pav	1 piece (30 g) + 1 Pav	2 ½ Carbohydrate, 2 Fat
Besan Chilla with Vegetables	1, 8″ diameter	2 Carbohydrate, 1 Protein, 1 Fat

Food	Amount	Composition
Bhindi (Okra) Masala	½ cup	1 Carbohydrate, 1 Fat
Appe with Coconut Chutney	2 each + 2 tbsp Chutney	1 ½ Carbohydrate, 2 Fat
Burrito, Vegetable/Bean	1, 5 oz (100 g)	3 Carbohydrate, 1 Protein, 2 Fat
Cabbage with Chana Dal Sabzi or Kootu	¾ cup	1 Carbohydrate, 1 Fat
Casseroles, Vegetable Homemade	1 cup (8 oz)	2 Carbohydrate, 1 Protein, 2 Fat
Chana or Chole Masala	½ cup	1 Carbohydrate, 1 Protein, 1 Fat
Chole Bhature	½ cup Chole + 1, 6" Bhatura	3 Carbohydrate, 1 Protein, 3 Fat
Chole Pindi	½ cup	1 Carbohydrate, 1 Protein, 1 Fat
Chole Puri	½ cup Chole + 2, 4" Puri	3, Carbohydrate, 1 Protein, 3 Fat
Chicken Nuggets, Soy-Based	2 Pieces (1 ½ oz)	½ Carbohydrate, 1 Protein, 1 Fat
Chinese Chow Mein Noodles with Vegetables	½ cup	1 Carbohydrate, 2 Fat

Food	Amount	Composition
Chinese Lo Mein Noodles with Vegetables	½ cup	1 Carbohydrate, 1 Fat
Dahi Vada	1 Vada (3/4") + 2 Tbsp Dahi (Yogurt)	1 ½ Carbohydrate, 1 Protein, 1 Fat
Dal (Lentils) Cooked with Tomatoes, Onions	½ cup	1 Carbohydrate, 1 Protein, 1 Fat
Thin Mixed Dal, Cooked	1 cup	1 Carbohydrate, 1 Protein, 1 Fat
Tomato Dal	½ cup	1 Carbohydrate, 1 Protein, 1 Fat
Dal Vada with Cilantro Chutney	2 Vadas, 1.0" diameter	1 Carbohydrate, 1 Protein, 1 Fat
Dhansak (Vegetarian)	1 cup	2 Carbohydrate, 1 Protein, 2 Fat
Dosa Plain with Sambhar and Coconut Chutney	1, 10" diameter Dosa, ½ cup Sambhar, 2 Tbsp Chutney	2 Carbohydrate, 1 Protein, 2 Fat
Dosa Masala with Aloo Sabzi	1, 8" diameter Dosa + ½ cup Sabzi	2 Carbohydrate, 2 Fat
Dosa Neer with Sambhar and Coconut Chutney	1, 10" diameter Dosa, ½ cup Sambhar, 2 Tbsp Chutney	3 Carbohydrate, 1 Protein, 2 Fat
Dosa, Rava Masala with Aloo Sabzi	1, 6" diameter Dosa + ½ cup Sabzi	2 Carbohydrate, 2 Fat
Falafel (Spiced Chickpea and Wheat Patties)	3 patties (2" across)	1 Carbohydrate, 1 Protein, 2 Fat
Farasbi Aloo Sabzi (Green Beans and Potatoes)	½ cup	1 Carbohydrate, 1 Fat
Farsabi Matar Sabzi (Green Beans and Peas)	½ cup	1 Carbohydrate, 1 Fat
Hot Dog, Soy-Based	1 (1½ oz)	½ Carbohydrate, 1 Protein, 1 Fat
Hummus with Pita	⅓ cup + ½, 6" diameter	2 Carbohydrate, 1 Protein, 1 Fat

Food	Amount	Composition
Idli with Coconut Chutney	1 small, 3" round + 1 Tbsp Chutney	2 Carbohydrate, 1 Protein, 1 ½ Fat
Idli with Sambhar	1 small, 3" round + ½ cup Sambhar	2 Carbohydrate, 1 Protein, 1 Fat
Idli Mini with Sambhar	5 each + ½ cup Sambhar	2 Carbohydrate, 1 Protein, 1 Fat
Jhunka	⅓ cup	1 ½ Carbohydrate, 1 Protein, 2 ½ Fat
Jhunka Bhakri	¾, 6" diameter Bhakri + ⅓ cup Jhunka	2 ½ Carbohydrate, 1 Protein, 2 ½ Fat
Kaddu, Lauki, Parwal, Tumba (Gourd) Sabzi with Chana Dal	¾, cup	1 Carbohydrate, 1 Fat
Kadhi, Gujarati	1 cup	1 Carbohydrate, 1 Protein, 1 Fat
Kadhi, Punjabi made with Besan (Chickpea Flour)	1 cup	2 Carbohydrate, 1 Protein, 1 Fat
Kadhi, Pakode Punjabi	½ cup	1 ½ Carbohydrate, 1 Protein, 1 Fat
Kadhi Chawal (Rice)	1 cup + ⅓ cup Rice	2 Carbohydrate, 1 Protein, 1 Fat
Kachumber, Koshimbir, Kosimbiri (Tomato and Onion with Yogurt)	1 cup	1 Carbohydrate, 1 Fat, 1 Protein
Lasagna with Vegetables	1 (3"x4")	2 Carbohydrate, 1 Protein, 2 Fat
Macaroni and Cheese	1 cup (8 oz)	2 Carbohydrate, 2 Proteins, 2 Fat
Macaroni and Pasta Salad	½ cup	2 Carbohydrate, 3 Fat
Makke di Roti and Sarson ka Saag	¾, 6" diameter Roti + ½ cup Saag	2 Carbohydrate, 1 Protein, 2 Fat

Food	Amount	Composition
Matar Paneer (Peas and Cottage Cheese)	¾ cup	1 Carbohydrate, 1 Protein, 3 Fat
Meatless Burger, Soy-Based	3 oz	½ Carbohydrate, 1 Protein, 1 Fat
Meal Replacement Bar, Small	1 bar (1 ½ oz)	1 ½ Carbohydrate, 1 Protein, 1 Fat
Meal Replacement Bar, Large	1 bar, (2 oz)	2 Carbohydrate, 1 Protein, 1 Fat
Meal Replacement Shake (Reduced Calorie)	1 can (10-11 oz)	1 ½ Carbohydrate, 1 Protein, 1 Fat
Medu Vada with Sambhar	1 piece with ½ cup Sambhar	2 ½ Carbohydrate, 1 Protein, 2 Fat
Methi Pithla	⅓ cup	1 ½ Carbohydrate, 1 Protein, 2 Fat
Methi Sabzi with Besan	½ cup	2 Carbohydrate, 1 Protein, 2 Fat
Methi Sabzi with Chana Dal	¾ cup	1 Carbohydrate, 1 Fat
Missal/Usal Pav	½ cup Missal+ 1 Pav	2 Carbohydrate, 1 Protein, 1 Fat
Momos, Vegetable	3 pieces	1 Carbohydrate, ½ Protein
Pachadi, Vellarika (Cucumber)	1 cup	1 Carbohydrate, 2 Fat

Food	Amount	Composition
Palak Dal (Spinach and Lentils)	½ cup	1 Carbohydrate, 1 Protein, ½ Fat
Palak Paneer Sabzi (Spinach and Paneer)	¾ cup	1 Carbohydrate, 2 Protein, 2 Fat
Paneer Bhurji	1 cup	1 Carbohydrate, 2.5 Protein, 3 Fat
Paneer Kadhai	1 cup	1 Carbohydrate, 2 Protein, 4 Fat
Paneer Tikka	¼ cup (2 oz)	½ Carbohydrate, 1 Protein, 2 Fat
Paneer Tikka Masala	½ cup	1 Carbohydrate, 1 Protein, 3 Fat
Paratha Aloo (Potato)	¾, 6″ diameter	1 Carbohydrate, 1 Fat
Paratha Gobi (Cauliflower)	¾, 6″ diameter	1 Carbohydrate, 1 Fat
Paratha Methi or Thepla (Fenugreek)	1, 6″ diameter	1 Carbohydrate, 1 Fat
Paratha Mooli (Radish)	1, 6″ diameter	1 Carbohydrate, 1 Fat
Paratha Palak (Spinach)	1, 6″ diameter	1 Carbohydrate, 1 Fat
Paratha Paneer	½, 6″ diameter	1 Carbohydrate, 1 Protein, 1 Fat
Parippu (Split Green Pea Fritters) with Cilantro Chutney	1, 2″ patty	1 Carbohydrate, 1 Protein, 2 Fat
Pav Bhaji: Pav (Dinner Roll) Bhaji	 1 ½ cup	2 Carbohydrate, 2 Fat
Pithla	⅓ cup	1 ½ Carbohydrate, 1 Protein, 2 Fat
Pithla Bhakri	¾, 6″ diameter Bhakri + ⅓ cup Pithla	2 ½ Carbohydrate, 1 Protein, 2 Fat
Pizza -Cheese with Regular Crust -Cheese with Thin Crust	¼ of a 10″ or 1/8 of 14″ (4 oz)	2 ½ Carbohydrate, 2 Proteins, 2 Fat 1½ Carbohydrate, 1 Protein, 2 Fat
Poriyal, Cabbage Fry	1 cup	1 Carbohydrate, 1 Fat
Poriyal, Green Beans Fry	1 cup	1 Carbohydrate, 1 Fat
Potato Salad	½ cup	2 Carbohydrate, 2 Fat
Puran Poli, Hollge, Vermi, Lanchipoli, Bobbatlu	½, 6″ diameter	1 Carbohydrate, 1 Protein, 1 Fat

Food	Amount	Composition
Quesadilla, Cheese	5 oz	2 Carbohydrate, 2 Proteins, 2 Fat
Raita, Boondi	½ cup	2 Carbohydrate, 1 Protein, 1 ½ Fat
Raita, Cucumber	1 cup	1 Carbohydrate, 1 Protein, 1 Fat
Raita, Vegetable	1 cup	1 Carbohydrate, 1 Protein, 1 Fat
Raita, Aloo (Potato)	½ cup	2 Carbohydrate, 1 Protein, 1 Fat
Rajma Chawal (Rice with Kidney Beans)	⅓ cup Rice + ½ cup Rajma	2 Carbohydrate, 1 Protein, 1 Fat
Rajma Curry	½ cup	1 Carbohydrate, 1 Protein, 1 Fat
Ravioli, Cheese	1 cup	2 Carbohydrate, 1 Protein, 1 Fat
Rice, Bisi Bhele Bhath	⅓ cup	1 Carbohydrate, 1 Protein, 1 Fat
Rice, Biryani/Pulao with Vegetables	½ cup	1 Carbohydrate, 1 Protein, 1 Fat
Rice with Dal (Lentils-Toor, Moong or Masoor)	⅓ cup Rice + ½ cup Dal	2 Carbohydrate, 1 Protein, 1 Fat
Rice, Coconut	⅓ cup	1 Carbohydrate, 1 Fat
Rice Flakes, (Poha) with Vegetables	½ cup	1 Carbohydrate, 1 Fat
Rice Flakes, (Poha) with Potatoes	½ cup	1 ½ Carbohydrate, 1 Fat
Rice, Kheer	½ cup	2 Carbohydrate, 2 Fat
Rice, Khichadi with Moong Dal	½ cup	1 Carbohydrate, 1 Protein, 1 Fat

Food	Amount	Composition
Rice, Khichadi with Vegetables	½ cup	1 Carbohydrate, 1 Protein, 1 Fat
Rice, Lemon	⅓ cup	1 Carbohydrate, 1 Fat
Rice, Puliyogare	⅓ cup	1 Carbohydrate, 1 Fat
Rice, Sweet, Shakkara Pongal	⅓ cup	1 ½ Carbohydrate, ½ Protein, 1 Fat
Rice, Tamarind	⅓ cup	1 Carbohydrate, 1 Fat
Rice, Ven Pongal	⅓ cup	1 Carbohydrate, ½ Protein, 1 Fat
Sabudana Khichadi or Savory Tapioca with Potatoes	1 cup	2 Carbohydrate, 2 Fat
Sabudana Vada with Peanut Yogurt Chutney	1 piece (35 g) Vada + 2 Tbsp Chutney	2 Carbohydrate, 2 Fat
Sambhar	½ cup	1 Carbohydrate, 1 Protein, 1 Fat
"Sausage" Patties, Soy-Based	1 (1½oz)	½ Carbohydrate, 1 Protein, 1 Fat
Shrikand (Kesar, Amrakhand) with Puri	Shrikhand ¼ cup + Puri 1, 4" diameter	3 Carbohydrate, 1 Protein, 2 Fat
Soups		
-Bean	½ cup (8 oz)	1 Carbohydrate, 1 Protein
-Chowder (made with milk)	1 cup (8 oz)	1 Carbohydrate, 1 Protein, 1 ½ Fat
-Cream (made with water)	1 cup (8 oz)	1 Carbohydrate, 1 Protein, 1 Fat
-Lentil	½ cup (4 oz)	1 Carbohydrate, 1 Protein
-Matzo Ball	1 cup (8 oz)	1 Carbohydrate, 1 Protein, 1 Fat
-Miso	1 cup (8 oz)	½ Carbohydrate, 1 Protein
-Mulligatawny	½ cup (4 oz)	1 Carbohydrate, 1 Protein, 1 Fat
-Ramen Noodle	1 cup (8 oz)	1 Carbohydrate
-Rice Soup/Kanji	1 cup (8 oz)	1 Carbohydrate
-Split Pea (made with water)	½ cup (4 oz)	1 Carbohydrate, 1 Protein
-Vegetable Noodle	1 cup (8 oz)	1 Carbohydrate
Spinach and Garbanzo Beans Curry	¾ cup	2 Carbohydrate, 1 Protein, 1 Fat
Tabbouleh, Parsley and Tomatoes	¾ cup	1 Carbohydrate, ½ Protein, 1 Fat
Tostada or Taco with Beans, Lettuce and Tomatoes	1 small	2 Carbohydrate, 1 Protein, 1 Fat
Undhiyu	½ cup	1 Carbohydrate, 1 Fat

Food	Amount	Composition
Upma (Cooked) Semolina with Vegetables	½ cup	1 Carbohydrate, 1 Fat
Upma Seviyan (Vermicelli) with Vegetables	½ cup	1 Carbohydrate, ½ Protein, 1 Fat
Uttapam, Vegetable or Mini Uttapam	1, 4" diameter	1 Carbohydrate, 1 Fat
Uttapam, Plain	1, 4" diameter	1 Carbohydrate, 1 Fat
Vegetable Korma	½ cup	1 ½ Carbohydrate, 1 Protein, 1 Fat
Vegetable Tofu Stir Fry	1 cup	2 Carbohydrate, 1 Protein, 2 Fat

Combination Foods: Non-Vegetarian

The Combination Foods list contains foods commonly consumed by the South Asian population. The amount of calories from carbohydrate and fat varies depending on the food consumed.

Non-Vegetarian Foods

15g Carbohydrate (1 Carbohydrate choice), 7g Protein (1 Protein choice), and 5g Fat (1 Fat choice)

Food	Amount	Composition
Aloo Gosht or Meat & Potato Salan/Curry	1 cup (2 oz meat)	1 ½ Carbohydrate, 2 Proteins, 2 Fat
Amritsari Machli (Fish Curry)	4oz (3 oz meat)	1 ½ Carbohydrate, 3 Proteins, 2 Fat
Anda Bhurji, Akuri (Spiced Scrambled Eggs with Vegetables)	1 cup	1 Carbohydrate, 2 Proteins,2 Fat
Breakfast Sandwiches -Biscuits, Eggs, Cheese, Bacon -Biscuits, Sausage -Burrito, Eggs, Cheese, Sausage -English Muffin, Eggs, Cheese, Meat	 1, 5 oz 1, 4 oz 1, 4 oz 1, 5 oz	 2 Carbohydrate, 3 Proteins, 3 Fat 2 Carbohydrate, 2 Proteins, 3 Fat 2 Carbohydrate, 3 Proteins, 3 Fat 2 Carbohydrate, 3 Proteins, 2 Fat
Burrito, Meat	1, 5 oz	2 Carbohydrate, 2 Proteins, 2 Fat
Casseroles with Meat, Homemade	1 cup (8 oz)	2 Carbohydrate, 2 Proteins, 2 Fat
Butter Chicken Curry	1 cup (3 oz meat)	1 Carbohydrate, 3 Proteins, 3 Fat
Chicken Chettinad Curry	1 cup (3 oz meat)	1 Carbohydrate, 3 Proteins, 3 Fat
Chicken Curry	1 cup (3 oz meat)	1 Carbohydrate, 3 Proteins, 3 Fat

Food	Amount	Composition
Chicken Do Piaza	1 cup (3 oz meat)	1 Carbohydrate, 3 Proteins, 2 Fat
Chicken Drumstick,		
Breaded and Baked	1, 3 oz	½ Carbohydrate, 2 Proteins, 2 Fat
Breaded and Fried	1, 3 oz	½ Carbohydrate, 2 Proteins, 3 Fat
Chicken Keema Matar	1 cup (3 oz meat)	1 Carbohydrate, 3 Proteins, 2 Fat
Chicken Kolhapuri	1 cup (3 oz meat)	1 Carbohydrate, 3 Proteins,2 Fat
Chicken, Lahori Charga	1 cup (4 oz)	½ Carbohydrate, 3 Proteins, 2 Fat
Chicken Manchurian	1 cup (4 oz)	1 Carbohydrate, 3 Proteins, 2 Fat
Chicken Mughlai	1 cup (3 oz meat)	1 Carbohydrate, 3 Proteins,3 Fat
Chicken Nuggets		
Fried	6-7 pieces	1 Carbohydrate, 2 Proteins, 3 Fat
Baked	6-7 pieces	1 Carbohydrate, 2 Proteins, 1 Fat
Orange Chicken (with Sweet Sauce)	1 cup	3 Carbohydrate, 2 Proteins, 3 Fat
Chicken Parmesan and Pasta	½ cup Pasta, 3 oz Meat	2 Carbohydrate, 3 Proteins, 3 Fat
Chicken Pot Pie	1- 7 oz pie	3 Carbohydrate, 1 Protein, 3 Fat
Chicken Quesadilla	5 oz	2 Carbohydrate, 3 Proteins, 2 Fat
Chicken and Rice	½ cup	1 Carbohydrate, 2 Proteins, 1 Fat
Chicken Seekh	1 cup (4 oz)	½ Carbohydrate, 3 Proteins, 2 Fat
Chicken, Sweet and Sour	¾ cup (6 oz)	1½ Carbohydrate, 2 Proteins, 3 Fat
Chicken 65	1 cup (3 oz meat)	1 Carbohydrate, 3 Proteins,2 Fat

Food	Amount	Composition
Chicken Tandoori	1 cup (4 oz)	½ Carbohydrate, 3 Proteins, 2 Fat
Chicken Tikka Masala	1 cup (3 oz meat)	1 Carbohydrate, 3 Proteins, 3 Fat
Chicken Tikka	1 cup (4 oz)	½ Carbohydrate, 3 Proteins, 2 Fat
Chicken Wing Baked Fried	1 Wing	1 Protein, 1 Fat 1 Protein, 2 Fat
Chili con Carne (Meat, Bean)	1 cup	2 Carbohydrate, 2 Proteins, 2 Fat
Chinese Chow Mein Noodles with Beef, Chicken or Pork	½ cup	1 Carbohydrate, 2 Proteins, 2 Fat
Chinese Lo Mein Noodles with Beef, Chicken or Pork	½ cup	1 Carbohydrate, 2 Proteins, 1 Fat
Dal Gosht or Meat & Dal Curry	1 cup	2 Carbohydrate, 3 Proteins, 3 Fat
Dhansak (Vegetables, Meat)	1 cup	2 Carbohydrate, 3 Proteins, 3 Fat
Egg Curry with 1 Egg	1 cup	1 Carbohydrate, 1 Protein, 2 Fat
Egg Roll with Chicken Egg Roll with Meat Egg Roll with Shrimp	1, 3 oz 1, 3 oz 1, 3 oz	1 ½ Carbohydrate, 1 Protein, 2 Fat 1 ½ Carbohydrate, 1 Protein, 2 Fat 1 ½ Carbohydrate, 1 Protein, 2 Fat
Empanada, Baked with Meat	1 medium	1 Carbohydrate, 1 Protein, 2 Fat
Fish Sticks Breaded and Baked Breaded and Fried	2, 1 oz each 2, 1 oz each	1 Carbohydrate, 1 Protein, 1 Fat 1 Carbohydrate, 1 Protein, 2 Fat
Goan Fish Curry (with 3 oz Pomfret, Mackerel, Shrimp, or Prawn)	1 cup	1 Carbohydrate, 3 Proteins, 3 Fat
Goan Fish Fry	3 oz	1 Carbohydrate, 2 Proteins, 3 Fat
Goat Curry (with 3 oz meat)	1 cup	1 Carbohydrate, 3 Proteins, 2 Fat
Goat/Lamb Keema Matar (3 oz meat)	1 cup	1 Carbohydrate, 3 Proteins, 3 Fat
Kadhai Goat Curry (3 oz meat)	1 cup	1 Carbohydrate, 3 Proteins, 2 Fat
Haleem (with Wheat/Lentils, 3oz Beef)	1 cup	2 Carbohydrate, 3 Proteins, 3 Fat

Food	Amount	Composition
Hamburger, Regular with Ketchup, Mustard, Onions	1- 2 oz Bun 4 oz Meat	2 Carbohydrate, 4 Proteins, 2 Fat
Cheeseburger with Ketchup, Mustard, Onions	1- 2 oz Bun, 4 oz Meat, 1 oz Cheese	3 Carbohydrate, 4 Proteins, 2 Fat
Hot Dog Plain with Bun	1- 2 oz Bun 1.6 oz Meat	2 Carbohydrate, 2 Proteins, 2 Fat
Hot Dog with Chili	1- 2 oz Bun 1.6 oz Hot Dog Meat, 1 oz Chili	2 Carbohydrate, 3 Proteins, 3 Fat
Kadhai Gosht (with 3 oz Beef)	1 cup	1 Carbohydrate, 3 Proteins, 3 Fat
Keema (Chicken, Goat or Lamb)	Pav 1 cup Keema, 1 Pav	2 Carbohydrates, 3 Proteins, 3 Fat
Lamb Chops (3 oz Meat)	1 cup (4 oz)	½ Carbohydrate, 3 Proteins, 2 Fat
Lamb Curry (3 oz Meat)	1 cup	½ Carbohydrate, 3 Proteins, 3 Fat
Lamb Kebab:		
Boti	1 cup (4 oz)	½ Carbohydrate, 3 Proteins, 2 Fat
Chappli	4 oz	½ Carbohydrate, 3 Proteins, 2 Fat
Seekh	1 cup (4 oz)	½ Carbohydrate, 3 Proteins, 2 Fat
Shami	4 oz	½ Carbohydrate, 3 Proteins, 2 Fat
Lamb Kofta Curry (3 oz Meat)	1 cup	1 Carbohydrate, 3 Proteins, 3 Fat
Lasagna with Meat Sauce	1 (3"x4")	2 Carbohydrate, 2 Proteins, 3 Fat
Momos, Meat or Poultry	3 pieces	1 Carbohydrate, 1 Proteins, 1 Fat
Mutton Curry (3 oz Meat)	1 cup	1 Carbohydrate, 3 Proteins, 2 Fat

Food	Amount	Composition
Mutton Korma (3 oz Meat)	1 cup	1 Carbohydrate, 3 Proteins, 2 Fat
Nachos with Cheese	8 pieces with 1 oz Cheese	2 Carbohydrate, 1 Protein, 2 Fat
Nihari (3 oz Meat)	1 cup	1 Carbohydrate, 3 Proteins, 2 Fat
Pizza		
Meat and Vegetable Combo	¼ of a 10" or 1/8 of 14" (4 oz)	2 ½ Carbohydrate, 2 Proteins, 3 Fat
Pepperoni, Regular Crust		2 ½ Carbohydrate, 2 Proteins, 3 Fat
Sausage, Regular Crust		2 ½ Carbohydrate, 2 Proteins, 3 Fat
Pepperoni, Thin Crust		1 ½ Carbohydrate, 2 Proteins, 3 Fat 1
Sausage, Thin Crust		½ Carbohydrate, 2 Proteins, 3 Fat
Pork Vindaloo (3 oz Meat)	1 cup	1 Carbohydrate, 3 Proteins, 2 Fat
Ravioli, Meat and Cheese	1 cup	2 Carbohydrate, 2 Proteins, 2 Fat
Rice, Biryani/Pulao with Meat	½ cup	1 Carbohydrate, 2 Proteins, 1 Fat
Rogan Josh (Chicken or Lamb)	1 cup	1 Carbohydrate, 3 Proteins, 3 Fat
Saag Gosht (Chicken or Lamb)	1 cup	½ Carbohydrate, 3 Proteins, 3 Fat
Sandwich	2 oz Bread	
Deli Meats	3 oz Meat	2 ½ Carbohydrate, 3 Proteins, 2 Fat
Breaded Fish Fillet	3 oz Fillet	3 Carbohydrate, 3 Proteins, 2 Fat
Chicken Salad	½ cup (3 ½ oz)	2 ½ Carbohydrate, 2 Proteins, 2 Fat
Crispy Chicken Fillet	3 oz Fillet	3 Carbohydrate, 3 Proteins, 3 Fat
Grilled Chicken Fillet	3 oz Fillet	3 Carbohydrate, 3 Proteins, 2 Fat
Ham and Cheese	2 oz Meat, 1 oz Cheese	2 ½ Carbohydrate, 3 Proteins, 2 Fat
Tuna Salad	½ cup (3 ½ oz)	2 ½ Carbohydrate, 2 Proteins, 2 Fat
Soups		
Beef Vegetable	1 cup	1 Carbohydrate, 1 Protein, 1 Fat
Chicken Noodle Soup	1 cup	1 Carbohydrate, 1 Protein, 1 Fat
Hot and Sour Soup	1 cup	½ Carbohydrate, ½ Fat
Spaghetti with Meatballs (3 oz Meat)	1 cup	2 Carbohydrate, 3 Proteins, 2 Fat
Stew, Meat and Vegetables	1 cup	1 Carbohydrate, 3 Proteins, 2 Fat
Submarine Sandwich	1, 6" Sub 4 oz Meat	3 Carbohydrate, 4 Proteins, 4 Fat
Taco Crisp with Meat, Cheese	1 small (3 oz)	1 Carbohydrate, 2 Proteins, 1 Fat

Food	Amount	Composition
Taco Salad with Chicken and Tortilla Bowl	1 Tortilla Bowl 4 oz Chicken, 1 oz Cheese	3 ½ Carbohydrate, 4 Proteins, 4 Fat
Tortellini, Meat and Cheese	¾ cup (3oz)	2 Carbohydrate, 2 Proteins, 2 Fat
Tostada with Meat, Beans, Cheese, Lettuce, Tomatoes	1 small	2 Carbohydrate, 2 Proteins, 1 Fat
Wraps, Grilled Chicken, Vegetables, Cheese, Sauce	1 Small Wrap (4-5 oz) with 3 oz Meat, 1 oz Cheese	2 Carbohydrate, 2 Proteins, 2 Fat

Snack Foods

The snack foods list contains commonly consumed snacks consumed by the South Asian population.

15g Carbohydrate (1 Carbohydrate choice) and 5g Fat (1 Fat choice)

Food	Amount	Composition
Aloo (Potato) Tikki	1, 3″ round	1 Carbohydrate, 1 Fat
Aloo Tikki Chaat	1, 3″ round	2 Carbohydrate, 2 Fat
Animal Crackers	8 crackers	1 Carbohydrate
Bakarwadi, Chitale Bandhu	1 oz	1 Carbohydrate, 2 Fat
Bakarwadi, Mini	1 oz	1 Carbohydrate, 2 Fat
Banana Chips	1 oz	1 Carbohydrate, 2 Fat
Bhadang, Murmura (Puff Rice)	1 cup	1 Carbohydrate, 1 Fat
Bhelpuri	1 cup	1 ½ Carbohydrate, 1 Protein, 2 Fat
Bhujiya, Aloo or Bikaneri	½ cup (1 ½ oz)	1 Carbohydrate, 2 Fat
Bhujiya, Sev	½ cup (1 ½ oz)	1 Carbohydrate, 2 Fat
Bourbon Biscuits	2 pieces	1 Carbohydrate, 1 Fat
Chakli	1 medium (2″ round)	1 Carbohydrate, 2 Fat
Chivda, Fried Poha with Nuts	½ cup	1 Carbohydrate, ½ Protein, 2 Fat
Chivda, Roasted Poha with Nuts	½ cup	1 Carbohydrate, ½ Protein, 1 Fat
Crackers -Crispbreads -Round-butter type -Saltine-type -Sandwich-style, with filling -Whole-wheat regular -Ritz	 2-5 6 6 3 2-5 4-6 round	 1 Carbohydrate, 1 Fat 1 Carbohydrate, 1 Fat 1 Carbohydrate, 1 Fat 1 Carbohydrate, 1 Fat 1 Carbohydrate, 1 Fat 1 Carbohydrate, 1 Fat

Food	Amount	Composition
Crispy Tea Rusk - Chai Time Toast Just Baked	2 pieces	1 Carbohydrate, 1 Fat
Dahi Batata Sev Puri	½ cup	2 Carbohydrate, 3 Fat
Dal Vada	2 Vadas, 1.0" diameter	1 Carbohydrate, 1 Protein, 1 Fat
Dhokla, Khatta	1, 1" square	1 Carbohydrate, 1 Fat
Dhokla, Khaman	1, 3 x 2" square	1 Carbohydrate, 1 Fat
Digestive High Fiber Biscuit Britannia	1 piece	1 Carbohydrate, 1 Fat
French Fries	10 (2 oz)	1 Carbohydrate, 2 Fat
Fruit Snacks, Chewy	1 roll	1 Carbohydrate
Graham Crackers	3 squares, (2½" square)	1 Carbohydrate
Granola or Snack Bar	1 bar (1 oz)	1½ Carbohydrate, 1 Fat

Food	Amount	Composition
Granola or Snack Bar, Fat-Free	1 bar (1 oz)	2 Carbohydrate
Gathiya, Papdi	½ cup (1 ½ oz)	1 Carbohydrate, 2 Fat
Gathiya, Tikha Garvi Gujarat	½ cup (1 ½ oz)	1 Carbohydrate, 2 Fat
Handavo	1 piece (3/4" square)	1 Carbohydrate, 1 Fat
Kachori (Mung Dal)	1 (3/4" round)	1 Carbohydrate, 2 Fat
Kachori (Vegetable)	1 (3/4" round)	1 Carbohydrate, 2 Fat
Khandavi	6 pieces (½" roll)	1 Carbohydrate, 1 Fat
Khari Biscuits	4 pieces	1 Carbohydrate, 2 Fat
Makhana or Fox Nuts Spiced, Roasted	2/3 cup or 20 g	1 Carbohydrate, ½ Fat
Marie Biscuits Britannia Gold	4 pieces	1 Carbohydrate, 1 Fat
Matar Karanji (Pea Turnover)	1 piece	1 Carbohydrate, 2 Fat
Mathris (1" diameter)	2 thin	1 Carbohydrate, 2 Fat
Melba Toast	4 pieces (2"x 4")	1 Carbohydrate
Murruku	1 medium (2" round)	1 Carbohydrate, 2 Fat
Muthia	1 oz	1 Carbohydrate, 1 Fat
Namkeen/Nimco	½ cup (1 ½ oz)*	1 Carbohydrate, 2 Fat
Oyster crackers	20	1 Carbohydrate
Pakoda, Potato	3 pieces	1 Carbohydrate, 2 Fat
Pakoda, Spinach	3 pieces	1 Carbohydrate, 2 Fat
Pani Puri	6	1 Carbohydrate, 2 Fat
Papad, Roasted	2	1 Carbohydrate
Papad, Fried	2	1 Carbohydrate, 1 Fat
Papri Chaat	½ cup	1 Carbohydrate, 1 Fat
Parle-G Original Gluco Biscuits	4 pieces	1 Carbohydrate, 1 Fat
Popcorn, Plain or Low Fat	3 cup	1 Carbohydrate
Pretzels, Mini	14 pieces (¾ oz)	1 Carbohydrate, 1 Fat
Pretzels including Nuggets	7 pieces (¾ oz)	1 Carbohydrate, 1 Fat
Rice Cakes	2 pieces, 4"	1 Carbohydrate
Sabudana Vada, Baked	1 piece (30 g)	2 Carbohydrate, 1 Fat

Food	Amount	Composition
Sabudana Vada, Fried*	1 piece (35 g)	2 Carbohydrate, 2 Fat
Sev Puri Chaat	2 puris	1 Carbohydrate, 1 Fat
Sev, Tikha	½ cup (1 ½ oz)	1 Carbohydrate, 2 Fat
Snack chips -Baked -Potato -Regular -Tortilla	 15-20 (¾ oz) 9-13 (¾ oz) 9-13 (¾ oz) 9-13 (¾ oz)	 1 Carbohydrate, 1 Fat 1 Carbohydrate, 2 Fat 1 Carbohydrate, 2 Fat 1 Carbohydrate, 2 Fat
Sooji Toast, Britannia	2 pieces	1 Carbohydrate
Trail Mix -Candy and Nut-based -Dried fruit-based	 1 oz 1 oz	 1 Carbohydrate, 2 Fat 1 Carbohydrate, 1 Fat
Vanilla Wafers	5 pieces	1 Carbohydrate
Vegetable Cutlet	1, 3" round	1 Carbohydrate, 1 Fat
Vegetable Samosa	¾" (medium) 1 piece	2 Carbohydrate, 2 Fat
Vegetable Meat or Poultry	¾" (medium) 1 piece	1½ Carbohydrate, 1 Protein, 2 Fat
Veggie Sticks	38 Straws (1oz)	1 Carbohydrate, 1 ½ Fat

Cakes, Desserts, and Sweets

15g Carbohydrate (1 Carbohydrate choice) and 5g Fat (1 Fat choice)

Food	Amount	Composition
Angel Food Cake, Unfrosted	1/12 cake, 2 oz	2 Carbohydrate
Banana Nut Bread	1" wide slice (1 oz)	2 Carbohydrate, 1 Fat
Barfi, Milk-Based	1 piece, 1½" x 1½"	2 Carbohydrate, 3 Fat
Basundi	1/3 cup	1 Carbohydrate, 1 Protein, 1 Fat
Brownie, small, Unfrosted	1 1/4" square, 1oz	1 Carbohydrate, 1 Fat
Cake, Unfrosted	2" square	1 Carbohydrate, 1 Fat
Cake, Frosted	2" square	2 Carbohydrate, 1 Fat
Cake, Mawa	2" square	1 ½ Carbohydrate, 1 Protein, 2 Fat
Candy		
- Chocolate, Dark or Milk Type	1 oz	1 Carbohydrate, 2 Fat
- Hard	3 pieces	1 Carbohydrate
Cookie		
- Chocolate Chip	2 small (2¼")	1 Carbohydrate, 2 Fat
- Gingersnap	3 cookies	1 Carbohydrate, 1 Fat
- Plain	2 small	1 Carbohydrate, 1 Fat
- Plain, Fat Free	2 small	1 Carbohydrate
- Sandwich with crème filling	2 small (⅔ oz)	1 Carbohydrate, 2 Fat
- Sugar-free	3 small (¾-1 oz)	1 Carbohydrate, 1 Fat
- Vanilla wafer	5 pieces	1 Carbohydrate, 1 Fat
Cupcake, frosted	1 small (1¾ oz)	2 Carbohydrate, 1 Fat
Donut, plain cake	1 medium, 2 oz	1 ½ Carbohydrate, 2 Fat
Donut, glazed	1 medium, 2 oz	2 Carbohydrate, 2 Fat
Falooda	½ cup	2 Carbohydrate, 1 Protein, 2 Fat
Falooda Kulfi	½ piece or cup	1 Carbohydrate, 1 Protein, 2 Fat
Fruit Cobbler	½ cup (3½ oz)	3 Carbohydrate, 1 Fat
Frozen Pops	1	½ Carbohydrate

Food	Amount	Composition
Fruit Juice Bars, Frozen	1 Bar (3 oz)	1 Carbohydrate
Fruit Snacks, Chewy	1 Roll (3/4 oz)	1 Carbohydrate
Fruit Spreads, 100% fruit	1 ½ Tbsp	1 Carbohydrate
Gelatin, regular	1/2 cup	1 Carbohydrate
Ghevar	1 piece, 2" round	2 Carbohydrate, 2 Fat
Granola bar	1 bar	1 Carbohydrate, 1 Fat
Gulab Jamun	1 small	1 Carbohydrate, 1 Fat
Gujiya, Karanji with Coconut Filling	1 piece	1 ½ Carbohydrate, 2 Fat
Gujiya, Karanji with Mawa Filling	1 piece	2 Carbohydrate, 2 Fat
Halwa, Gajar (Carrot)	⅓ cup	1 Carbohydrate, 2 Fat
Halwa, Doodhi or Lauki (Bottle Gourd)	⅓ cup	1 ½ Carbohydrate, 1 Fat
Halwa, Suji, Sheera	¼ cup	1 Carbohydrate, 2 Fat
Honey	1 Tbsp	1 Carbohydrate
Jam or Jelly, Regular	1 Tbsp	1 Carbohydrate

Food	Amount	Composition
Kada, Karah Prasad	¼ cup	1 ½ Carbohydrate, 2 Fat
Kesari	¼ cup	1 Carbohydrate, 2 Fat
Kheer, Rice or Seviyan or Suji	½ cup	2 Carbohydrate, 2 Fat
Kulfi	½ cup	1 Carbohydrate, 2 Fat
Ice cream	1/2 cup	1 Carbohydrate, 2 Fat
Ice cream, light	1/2 cup	1 Carbohydrate, 1 Fat
Ice cream, Fat-free, no sugar added	1/2 cup	1 Carbohydrate
Laddoo, Rava	1 small	1 Carbohydrate, 1 Fat
Laddoo, Atta/Besan	1 small	1 Carbohydrate, 2 Fat
Magas	1 piece, 1½" x 1½"	2 Carbohydrate, 3 Fat
Modak, Fried	1 piece, 1½" x 1½"	2 ½ Carbohydrate, 1 Fat
Modak, Steamed	1 piece, 1½" x 1½"	2 ½ Carbohydrate, 1 Fat
Mohanthal	1 piece, 1 ½" x 1 ½"	1 ½ Carbohydrate, 1 Fat
Syrup		
- Agave	1 Tbsp	1 Carbohydrate
- Chocolate	2 Tbsp	2 Carbohydrate
- Maple Syrup Light	2 Tbsp	1 Carbohydrate
- Maple Syrup Regular	1 Tbsp	1 Carbohydrate
- Pancake Syrup Light	2 Tbsp	1 Carbohydrate
- Pancake Syrup	1 Tbsp	1 Carbohydrate
Muffin	¼ muffin (1 oz)	1 Carbohydrate, 1 Fat
Nankhatai	2 small	1 Carbohydrate, 1 Fat
Payasam	½ cup	2 Carbohydrate, 2 Fat
Pesarapappu Payasam	½ cup	2 Carbohydrate, 2 Fat
Petha, Pumpkin/Gourd	1 piece, 1" square	2 Carbohydrate
Phirni (Plain or Mango)	½ cup	2 Carbohydrate, 2 Fat
Pie, Fruit, 2 Crusts	1/6 pie	3 Carbohydrate, 2 Fat
Pie, Pumpkin or Custard	1/8 pie	1 Carbohydrate, 2 Fat
Pudding, Regular, with Low Fat Milk	1/2 cup	2 Carbohydrate
Pudding, Sugar-Free, Low-Fat Milk	1/2 cup	1 Carbohydrate
Rabdi	¼ cup	2 Carbohydrate, 2 Fat, 1 Protein
Rasgulla	1 medium (50 g)	2 Carbohydrate
Rasmalai		
-Nanak	1 piece (80 g)	1 Carbohydrate, 2 Fat
-Haldiram's	1 piece (83 g)	1 Carbohydrate, 3 Fat
Rice, Sweet, Shakkara Pongal	⅓ cup	1 ½ Carbohydrate, ½ Protein, 1 Fat
Sherbet, Sorbet	1/2 cup	2 Carbohydrate

Food	Amount	Composition
Shrikand, Kesar	¼ cup (50 g)	1 ½ Carbohydrate, 1 Fat
Shrikhand, Mango (Amrakhand)	¼ cup (50 g)	1 ½ Carbohydrate, 1 Fat
Sweet Roll or Danish	1 (2 ½ oz)	2 ½ Carbohydrate, 2 Fat
Yogurt, frozen, - Low Fat, Fat-free - Low Fat with Fruit - Regular	 ⅓ cup ½ cup ½ cup	 1 Carbohydrate 2 Carbohydrate, 0-1 Fat 1 Carbohydrate, 1 Fat

Sugars

15g Carbohydrate (1 Carbohydrate choice)

Food	Amount	Composition
Blended Sweeteners (Mixture of Artificial Sweeteners and Sugar)	1 Tbsp	1 Carbohydrate
Sugar	1 tsp	1 Carbohydrate

Beverages, Soda, and Energy/Sports Drinks

15g Carbohydrate (1 Carbohydrate choice)

Food	Amount	Composition
Cranberry Juice Cocktail	½ cup	1 Carbohydrate
Energy Drink	1 can (8.3 oz)	2 Carbohydrate
Fruit Drink or Lemonade	1 cup (8 oz)	2 Carbohydrate
Hot Chocolate, Regular (Envelope) Hot Chocolate, Sugar-free or Light (Envelope)	1, 1 cup water 1, 1 cup water	1 Carbohydrate + 1 Fat 1 Carbohydrate
Rooh Afza	3 Tbsp, 1 cup water	1 ½ Carbohydrae
Soft drink (soda), regular	1 can (12 oz)	2 ½ Carbohydrate
Sports drink	1 cup (8 oz)	1 Carbohydrate

Proteins

Each serving of protein (meats, poultry, fish, eggs, cheese, and plant-based) on this list contains about 7 grams of protein. The total amount of Calories varies depending on the amount of fat in the meat chosen. The list is divided into very lean protein, lean protein, medium-fat protein, and high-fat protein. One ounce of meat, poultry, fish, or cheese is equivalent to 1 protein choice.

	Carbohydrate (g)	Protein (g)	Fat (g)	Calories
Very Lean Protein	0	7	0-1	35
Lean Protein	0	7	3	55
Medium-Fat Protein	0	7	5	75
High-Fat Protein	0	7	8	100
Plant-based Protein	varies	7	varies	varies

Very Lean Protein

One choice has 7g of protein, 0-1g of fat, and a total of 35 Calories

*Count as One carbohydrate choice and One very lean protein choice

Food	Amount
Cheese with 0-1 g Fat: Fat-Free Cottage-Cheese, Non-Fat or Low-Fat Paneer, 1% Milk	 1 oz ¼ cup ¼ cup (2 oz)
Clams (Tisrya) or Mussels	9 each
Cooked Peas, Beans, Pulses or Legumes (Dal)*	½ cup
Egg: Egg Substitutes Egg whites	 ¼ cup 2
Fish, Fresh or Frozen: Cod, Flounder, Haddock, Halibut, King Fish (Surmai), Milk Fish, Orange Roughy, Pomfret (Paplet), Mackerel (Bangda), Tilapia, Trout, Tuna (Fresh or Canned in Water)	1 oz 1 oz
Game: Buffalo, Duck or Pheasant (Skinless), Ostrich, Venison	1 oz
Goat Meat	1 oz
Hot Dog with 0-1 g Fat per oz	1
Organ Meats: Heart, Kidney, Liver (High Cholesterol)	1 oz
Poultry: Chicken or Turkey (White Meat, Skinless), Cornish Hen (Skinless)	1 oz
Processed Sandwich Meats with 0-1 gm Fat per oz: Chipped Beef, Deli Thin-Sliced Meats, Turkey Ham, Turkey Kielbasa, Turkey Pastrami	1 oz
Shellfish: Crab, Imitation Shellfish, Lobster, Shrimp	1 oz
Tofu, Light	4 oz (1/2 cup)

Lean Protein

One choice has 7g of protein, 3g of fat, and a total of 55 Calories

Food	Amount
Beef: Select or Choice Grade Ground Round, Roast (Chuck, Rib, Rump), Sirloin, Steak (Flank, Porterhouse, T-Bone, Cubed), Tenderloin	1 oz
Beef Jerky	1 oz
Cheeses with 3 g of Fat or less: Cheese Cottage Cheese, 4.5% Fat Parmesan, Grated	 1 oz ¼ cup 2 Tbsp
Fish: Catfish, Salmon (Fresh or Canned), Herring, Indian Salmon (Rawas) Smoked: Herring or Salmon (Lox) Sardines, Canned Tuna, Canned in oil Drained	 1 oz 1 oz 2 medium 1 oz
Hot Dogs with 3 grams or less Fat per oz	1
Game: Goose (Skinless), Rabbit	1 oz
Ground Meat Kebab	1 oz
Lamb: Chop, Leg, Roast	1 oz
Luncheon Meat with 3 grams or less Fat per oz	1 oz
Oysters, Fresh or Frozen	6 medium
Pork, Lean: Canned, Cured, or Fresh Ham, Pork Tenderloin, Canadian Bacon, Rib or Loin Chop	1 oz
Poultry: Chicken (White Meat with Skin), Chicken (Dark Meat, Skinless), Baked/Tandoori Chicken, Turkey (Dark Meat, Skinless), Domestic Duck or Goose (Well Drained of Fat, Skinless)	1 oz

Food	Amount
Sausage with 1-3 g Fat per oz	1 oz
Shrimp, Prawn (Kolambi, Jhinga) and Squid (High Cholesterol)	1 oz
Veal, Lean Veal, Lean Chop, Roast	1 oz

Medium-Fat Protein

One choice has 7g of protein, 5g of fat, and a total of 75 Calories

Food	Amount
Beef: Prime Grades such as Prime Rib, Ground Beef, Meatloaf, Corned Beef, Short Ribs	1 oz
Cheese: Feta, Mozzarella, Ricotta	1 oz
Poultry: Chicken (Dark Meat with Skin), Ground Turkey or Ground Chicken, Fried Chicken (With Skin)	1 oz
Chicken, Fish, Lamb Tikka	1 oz
Egg	1
Fish, Fried	1 oz
Lamb Rib, Roast, Ground	1 oz

Food	Amount
Pork Chops, Top Loin, Boston Butt, Cutlets	1 oz
Sausage with 5 grams or less Fat per oz	1
Soy Milk	1 cup
Tempeh	1 ½ oz (¼ cup)
Tofu	4 oz (1/2 cup)
Veal Cutlet (Unbreaded)	1 oz

High-Fat Protein

One choice has 7g of protein, 8g of fat, and a total of 100 Calories

Food	Amount
Bacon	3 Slices
Cheese: All Regular Cheeses such as American, Cheddar, Swiss, Monterey Jack Paneer, Regular	1 oz 1 ½ oz (1/4 cup)
Frankfurter (Turkey or Chicken)	1
Hot Dog	1 each
Peanut Butter	2 Tbsp
Pork: Spareribs, Sausage, Ground Pork	1 oz
Processed Sandwich Meats with 8 grams or less Fat per oz: Bologna, Pimento Loaf, Salami	1 oz
Sausage, such as Polish, Italian	1 oz

Plant-Based Protein

Carbohydrate content of plant-based proteins vary and Calories vary.

Food	Amount	Composition
"Bacon" Strips, Soy-based, Meatless Bacon,	2 strips (approx ½ oz)	1 Lean Protein
Baked Beans, Canned, Plain or Vegetarian	⅓ cup	1 Carbohydrate, 1 Lean Protein
Beans: Black, Cooked or Canned, Drained and Rinsed	½ cup	1 Carbohydrate, 1 Very Lean Protein
Beans: Garbanzo, Cooked or Canned, Drained and Rinsed	½ cup	1 Carbohydrate, 1 Very Lean Protein
Beans: Kidney, Cooked or Canned, Drained and Rinsed	½ cup	1 Carbohydrate, 1 Very Lean Protein
Beans: Navy, Cooked or Canned, Drained and Rinsed	½ cup	1 Carbohydrate, 1 Very Lean Protein
Edamame, Frozen	½ cup	½ Carbohydrate, 1 Very Lean Protein
Falafel	3 patties (about 2 inches across)	1 Carbohydrate, 1 High Fat Protein
Hummus	1/3 cup	1 Carbohydrate, 1 High-fat Protein
Lentils, Cooked	½ cup	1 Carbohydrate, 1 Very Lean Protein
Meatless Burger, Soy-based	1 patty (about 2½ oz)	½ Carbohydrate, 2 Very Lean Protein
Meatless Burger, Vegetable	1 patty (about 2½ oz)	½ Carbohydrate, 1 Very Lean Protein

Meatless Chicken	1/3 cup (2 oz)	½ Carbohydrate, 2 Lean Protein
Meatless Frankfurter	1(2½ oz)	2 High Fat Proteins
Meatless Luncheon Slices	1 slice (½ oz)	1 Very Lean Protein
Meatless Sausage	1 slice (1 oz)	1 Medium-Fat Protein
Nut Spreads: Almond Butter, Cashew Butter, Peanut Butter, Soy Nut Butter	1 Tbsp	1 High-fat Protein
Soy Nuts, unsalted	¾ oz	½ Carbohydrate, 1 Medium- fat Protein
Split Peas Cooked	½ cup	1 Carbohydrate, 1 Very Lean Protein
Refried Beans, Canned, Vegetarian	½ cup	1 Carbohydrate, 1 Lean Protein
Tempeh, Plain, Unflavored	¼ cup (1 ½ oz)	1 Medium-fat Protein
Tofu, Firm	½ cup (4 oz)	1 Medium-fat Protein
Tofu, Light	½ cup (4 oz)	1 Lean Protein

Fats

Fat is divided into unsaturated Fat (monounsaturated and polyunsaturated), saturated Fat, and trans-Fat.
One fat choice contains 5 grams of fat and 45 Calories.

Unsaturated Fat - Monounsaturated Fat

Food	Amount
Avocado, Medium (Makhanphal)	1/8 (1 oz)
Brazil Nuts	2 nuts
Filberts (Hazelnuts)	6 whole
Oil (Canola, Olive, Peanut)	1 tsp
Olives: Ripe (Black) Green, Stuffed	8 large 10 large
Macadamia Nuts	3 kernels (¼ oz)
Nut Butter: Almond Butter Cashew Butter Hazelnut Butter Macadamia Nut Butter Pecan Butter Pistachio Butter Walnut Butter	 2 tsp 2 tsp 2 tsp 2 tsp 2 tsp 2 tsp 2 tsp
Nuts: Almonds (Badam) Cashews (Kaju) Mixed (50% Peanuts)	 6 nuts 6 nuts 6 nuts
Peanuts (Mungphali, Shengdana)	10 nuts
Peanut Butter, Smooth or Crunchy	2 tsp

Pecans (Chota Akhrot)	4 halves
Pistachios (Pista)	18 kernels
Sesame Seeds (Til)	1 Tbsp
Tahini or Sesame Seed Butter	2 tsp
Walnuts (Akhrot)	4 halves

Unsaturated Fat - Polyunsaturated Fat

Food	Amount
Margarine, Trans Fat-Free (Stick, Tub, or Squeeze)	1 tsp
Margarine, Reduced-Fat Trans Fat-Free (30-50% vegetable oil)	1 Tbsp
Mayonnaise, Regular	1 tsp
Mayonnaise, Reduced-Fat	1 Tbsp
Miracle Whip, Regular	2 tsp
Miracle Whip, Light	1 Tbsp
Oil (Corn, Flaxseed, Grape Seed, Safflower, Soybean, Sunflower)	1 tsp
Pine Nuts (Pignolia)	1 Tbsp
Salad Dressings, Regular	1 Tbsp
Salad Dressings, Reduced-Fat	2 Tbsp
Seeds, Pumpkin or Sunflower	1 Tbsp
Pumpkin Seed Butter	1 Tbsp
Sunflower Seed Butter	1 Tbsp
Soy Butter	1 Tbsp
Soy Nuts, unsalted	¾ oz

Saturated Fat

Food	Amount
Butter, Stick Whipped	1 tsp 2 tsp
Butter, Reduced Fat	1 Tbsp
Bacon	1 Slice
Chitterlings, Boiled	2 Tbsp (½ oz)
Coconut, Shredded	2 Tbsp
Coconut Milk Light Regular	 1/3 cup 1½ Tbsp
Cream, Light or Half and Half	2 Tbsp
Cream, Sour, Regular	2 Tbsp
Cream, Sour, Reduced Fat	3 Tbsp
Cream, Heavy, Whipping	1 Tbsp
Cream Cheese, Regular	1 Tbsp
Cream Cheese, Reduced Fat	2 Tbsp
Ghee (Clarified Butter)	1 tsp
Lard	1 tsp
Oil (Coconut)	1 tsp
Oil (Palm, Palm Kernel)	1 tsp
Salt Pork	1/4 oz
Shortening, Solid	1 tsp

Trans Fat are created in an industrial process that adds hydrogen to liquid vegetable oils to make them more solid. Partially hydrogenated and hydrogenated Fat are types of processed Fat and should be avoided.

Free Foods

Foods like sugar-free sodas and beverages, artificial sweeteners, spices, and seasonings are included in this list. Free food is any food or drink that contains less than 20 Calories or less than 5 grams of carbohydrate per serving. For items that have no serving size specified, any amount may be used. *Items that have a serving size should not exceed three servings per day.*

Fat-free or Reduced-fat Foods contain < 5g carbs and 20 Calories

Food	Amount
Cream Cheese, Fat-Free	1 Tbsp
Coffee Creamers, Nondairy, Liquid	1 Tbsp
Coffee Creamers, Nondairy, Powdered	2 tsp
Margarine, Fat-Free	4 Tbsp
Margarine, Reduced-Fat	1 tsp
Mayonnaise, Fat-Free	1 Tbsp
Mayonnaise, Reduced-Fat	1 tsp
Non-Stick Cooking Spray, Salad Dressing, Mayonnaise-Type, Fat-Free	1 Tbsp
Salad Dressing, Mayonnaise-Type, Reduced Fat	1 tsp
Salad Dressing, Fat-Free	1 Tbsp
Salad Dressing, Fat-Free, Italian	2 Tbsp
Salsa	1/4 cup
Sour Cream, Fat-Free	1 Tbsp
Whipped Topping, Light or Fat-Free	2 Tbsp
Whipped Topping, Regular	1 Tbsp

Sugar-free or Low-Carbohydrate Foods contain < 5g carbs and 20 Calories

Food	Amount
Candy, Hard, Sugar-Free	1 candy
Cranberries or Rhubarb, Sweetened with Sugar Substitute	½ cup
Gelatin, Sugar-Free Gum, Sugar-Free Jam/Jelly, sugar-free	2 tsp
Pancake Syrup, Sugar-Free	2 Tbsp
Salad Greens (Arugula, Chicory, Endive, Escarole, Lettuce, Radicchio, Spinach, Watercress	
Sugar Substitute	
Vegetables, Cooked Non-Starchy	¼ cup
Vegetables, Raw Non- Starchy	½ cup

Drinks contain < 5g carbs and 20 Calories

Food	Amount
Bouillon or Broth without Fat Bouillon, ,	1 Tbsp
Cocoa Powder, Unsweetened	1 Tbsp
Low-Sodium Carbonated drinks	
Sugar-Free Club soda	
Coffee/tea Drink mixes, sugar-free Tonic water	

Condiments contain < 5g carbs and 20 Calories

Food	Amount
Balsamic Vinegar	1 Tbsp
Barbecue Sauce	2 tsp
Catsup, Ketchup	1 Tbsp
Chili Sauce, Sweet, Tomato-Type	2 tsp
Chunda (Mango Pickle)	1 tsp
Coconut Chutney	1 tsp
Cranberry Sauce, Jellied	1 tsp
Curry Sauce	1 tsp
Hoisin Sauce	1 tsp
Horseradish	2 tsp
Hot Pepper Sauce	2 tsp
Lemon or Lime juice	2 tsp
Miso	1 ½ tsp
Mustard Honey, Brown, Dijon, Yellow	1 Tbsp
Parmesan Cheese	1 Tbsp
Peri Peri Sauce	2 Tbsp
Pickles, Unsweetened	1 ½ large
Pickle Relish	1 Tbsp
Pimento	1 Tbsp
Plum Sauce	1 tsp
Salad Dressing, Fat-Free, Cream-Based	1 tsp
Salsa	¼ cup
Soy Sauce	1 Tbsp
Sweet and Sour Sauce	1 tsp
Tamarind Chutney	1 tsp
Taco Sauce	1 Tbsp
Vinegar	1 Tbsp

Worcestershire Sauce	1 Tbsp
Yogurt, Any Type	2 Tbsp

Free Snacks

These foods in these serving sizes are perfect free food snacks.

Food	Amount
Baby Carrots and Celery Sticks	5
Blueberries	¼ cup
Sliced Cheese, Fat-free	½ oz
Goldfish-Style Crackers	10
Saltine Type Crackers	1
Frozen Cream Pop, Sugar-free	1
Lean Meat	½ oz
Light Popcorn	1 cup
Vanilla Wafer	1

Drinks/Mixes

Any food on this list—without a serving size listed—can be consumed in any moderate amount.

Bouillon, Broth, Consomme	Diet Soft Drinks, Sugar-free
Bouillon or Broth, Low Sodium	Drink Mixes, Sugar-free
Carbonated or Mineral Water	Tea, Unsweetened or With Sugar Substitute
Club Soda	Tonic Water, Diet
Cocoa Powder, Unsweetened (1 Tbsp)	Water
Coffee, Unsweetened or With Sugar Substitute	Water, Flavored, Carbohydrate Free

Seasonings

Any food on this list can be consumed in any moderate amount.

Flavoring Extracts (For Example Vanilla, Almond, Peppermint)	Spices
Garlic	Hot Pepper Sauce
Herbs, Fresh or Dried	Wine, Used for Cooking
Nonstick Cooking Spray	Worcestershire Sauce
Pimento	

Alcohols

One alcohol equivalent or choice is defined as a ½ oz of absolute alcohol and comprises 100 Calories. One carbohydrate choice is a serving of food that has 15 grams of Carbohydrates and comprises 80 Calories

Alcoholic Beverage	Serving Size	Count as
Beer		
Light (4.2%)	12 fl oz	1 alcohol equivalent + ½ carbohydrate
Regular (4.9%)	12 fl oz	1 alcohol equivalent + 1 carbohydrate
Dark (5.7%)	12 fl oz	1 alcohol equivalent + 1 – 1 ½ Carbohydrate
Distilled Spirits: Vodka, Rum, Gin, Whiskey, Tequila (80 or 86 proof)	1 ½ fl oz	1 alcohol equivalent
Liqueur, Coffee (53 proof)	1 fl oz	½ alcohol equivalent + 1 carbohydrate
Sake	1 fl oz	½ alcohol equivalent
Champagne/Sparkling	5 fl oz	1 alcohol equivalent
Dessert (Sherry)	3 ½ fl oz	1 alcohol equivalent + 1 carbohydrate
Dry, Red or White (10%)	5 fl oz	1 alcohol equivalent

1500 Calories Sample Menu Plan: North Indian Non-Vegetarian

Daily Calories = 1500 kcal

- Carbohydrates 195 g = 780 kcal (52% of total Calorie) = 13 Total Number of Carbohydrate Choices
- Protein 90 g = 360 kcal (24% of total Calories)
- Fat 40 g = 360 kcal (24% of total Calories)

Meal/Snack	Menu: Food and Serving Size	Number of Carbohydrate Choices
Breakfast Number of Carbohydrate Choices = 2	1 large Egg Omelet	0
	1 Slice Whole Grain Toast	1
	1 Small Banana	1
	2 tsp Butter	0
	1 Cup Chai (2% milk)	0
Morning Snack Number of Carbohydrate Choices = 1	1 oz (38 Straws) Veggie sticks	1
Lunch Number of Carbohydrate Choices = 4	¾ cup Matar Paneer Sabzi	1
	½ cup Red Kidney Beans (Rajma)	1
	2 Rotis, 6″ each	2
Afternoon Snack Number of Carbohydrate Choices =1	6 Almonds or Cashews or Mixed Nuts	1
Dinner Number of Carbohydrate Choices = 4	1 cup Chicken Curry	1
	1 Roti 6″	1
	1/3 cup cooked White/Brown Rice	1
	½ cup Aloo Gobi Sabzi	1
	½ cup Salad or Kachumber	0
Evening Snack Number of Carbohydrate Choices =1	1 cup 2% Milk	1
Daily Total Number of Carbohydrate Choices		13

1500 Calories Sample Menu Plan: South Indian Non-Vegetarian

Daily Calories = 1516 kcal

- 195 g Carbohydrates = 780 kcal (51% of total Calories) = 13 Total Number of Carbohydrate Choices
- 94 g Protein = 376 kcal (25% of total Calories)
- 40 g Fat = 360 kcal (24% of total Calories)

Meal/Snack	Menu: Food and Serving Size	Number of Carbohydrate Choices
Breakfast Number of Carbohydrate Choices = 2	Anda Bhurji (1 large egg)	0
	1 Slices Whole Grain Toast	1
	2 tsp butter	1
	1 cup Chai (2% milk)	0
Lunch Number of Carbohydrate Choices = 4	½ cup Sambar	1
	1 cup Cabbage Poriyal	1
	1 Roti, 6"	1
	1/3 cup Cooked White Rice	1
Afternoon Snack Number of Carbohydrate Choices = 1	6 Almonds or Cashews or Mixed nuts	1
Dinner Number of Carbohydrate Choices = 4	1 cup Chicken Chettinad Curry	1
	1 Roti 6"	1
	½ cup Rasam	0
	1 cup Low-fat yogurt	1
	1/3 cup cooked White/Brown Rice	1
Evening Snack Number of Carbohydrate Choices = 2	1 cup 2% Milk 1¼ Watermelon Cubes	1 1
Daily Total Number of Carbohydrate Choices		**13**

1500 Calories Sample Menu Plan: North Indian Vegetarian

Daily Calories = 1524 kcal

- 195 g Carbohydrates = 780 kcal (51% of total Calories) = 13 Total Number of Carbohydrate Choices
- 96 g Protein = 384 kcal (25% of total Calories)
- 40 g Fat = 360 kcal (24% of total Calories)

Meal/Snack	Menu: Food and Serving Size	Number of Carbohydrate Choices
Breakfast Number of Carbohydrate Choices = 3	1 6' Paneer Paratha or 2 Whole Wheat Toast with 2 tsp Butter	2
	⅔ cup Low-fat Yogurt	1
	1 cup Chai (2% milk)	0
Lunch Number of Carbohydrate Choices = 4	½ cup Toor dal cooked	1
	1 ½ cup Vegetable Tofu Stir Fry	1
	1/3 cup White/Brown Rice cooked	1
	1 Roti, 6"	1
Afternoon Snack Number of Carbohydrate Choices = 1	½ cup Sprouted Moong Salad	1
Dinner Number of Carbohydrate Choices = 3	½ cup Khichadi	1
	1 Roti	1
	½ cup Kadhi	1
	½ cup Okra (Bhindi) Masala	0
Evening Snack Number of Carbohydrate Choices = 2	1 cup 2% Milk	1
	6 Saltine-type Crackers	1
	1 tbsp Almond butter	0
Daily Total Number of Carbohydrate Choices		13

1500 Calories Sample Menu Plan: South Indian Vegetarian

Daily Calories = 1520 kcal

- 200 g Carbohydrates = 800 kcal (52% of total Calories) = 13.5 Total Number of Carbohydrate Choices
- 90 g Protein = 360 kcal (24% of total Calories)
- 40 g Fat = 360 kcal (24% of total Calories)

Meal/Snack	**Menu: Food and Serving Size**	**Number of Carbohydrate Choices**
Breakfast Number of Carbohydrate Choices = 3	2 Small Idli	2
	½ cup Sambar	1
	1 tbsp Tomato Chutney	0
	1 cup Chai (2% milk)	0
Lunch Number of Carbohydrate Choices = 4	½ cup Toor Dal Cooked	1
	½ cup Cabbage Poriyal	0
	⅔ cup White/Brown Rice cooked	2
	1 Roti	1
Afternoon Snack Number of Carbohydrate Choices = 1	2/3 cup Low-fat Yogurt	1
Dinner Number of Carbohydrate Choices = 4.5	1/3 cup Bisi Bhele Bath	1
	1 cup Cucumber Raita	1
	1 Roti	1
	½ cup Vegetable Korma	1.5
Evening Snack Number of Carbohydrate Choices = 1	6 Almonds or Cashews or Mixed Nuts	1
Daily Total Number of Carbohydrate Choices		13.5

1800 Calories Sample Menu Plan: North Indian Non-Vegetarian

Daily Calories = 1820 kcal

- 240g Carbohydrates = 960 kcal (53% of total Calories) = 16 Total Number of Carbohydrate Choices
- 108g Protein = 432 kcal (24% of total Calories)
- 48g Fat = 428 kcal (23% of total Calories)

Meal/Snack	Menu: Food and Serving Size	Number of Carbohydrate Choices
Breakfast Number of Carbohydrate Choices = 3	2 Eggs (white only) Omelet with Vegetables	0
	2 Slices Whole Grain toast	2
	2 tsp butter	0
	1 small Fruit	1
	1 cup Chai (2% milk)	0
Morning Snack Number of Carbohydrate Choices = 1	1 ½-2 tbsp Dry Berries (Trail mix)	1
Lunch Number of Carbohydrate Choices = 4	½ cup Matar Paneer	1
	½ cup Red Kidney Beans (Rajma)	1
	1 Roti, 6"	1
	1/3 cup cooked White/Brown rice	1
	½ cup Salad or Raita	0
Afternoon Snack Number of Carbohydrate Choices = 2	6 Almonds or Cashews or mix	1
	2/3 cup Low-Fat Fruit Yogurt	1

Dinner Number of Carbohydrate Choices = 4	1/2 cup Sprouted Moong Salad	1
	1 cup Chicken Curry	1
	1 Roti, 6″	1
	1/3 cup cooked White/Brown Rice	1
Evening Snack Number of Carbohydrate Choices = 2	1 cup 2% Milk	1
	6 Saltine-type crackers	1
Daily Total Number of Carbohydrate Choices		16

1800 Calories Sample Menu Plan: South Indian Non-Vegetarian

Daily Calories = 1830 kcal

- 240g Carbohydrates = 960 kcal (52% of total Calories) = 16 Total Number of Carbohydrate Choices
- 107g Protein = 428 kcal (23.5% of total Calories)
- 49g Fat = 441 kcal (24% of total Calories)

Meal/Snack	Menu: Food and Serving Size	Number of Carbohydrate Choices
Breakfast Number of Carbohydrate Choices = 3	Anda Bhurji (2 egg white only) with Vegetables	0
	2 Slices Whole Grain Toast	2
	2 tsp Butter	0
	1 small Fruit	1
	1 cup Chai (2% milk)	0
Morning Snack Number of Carbohydrate Choices = 1	3 Graham Crackers	1
	1oz Peanut/Almond Butter	0
Lunch Number of Carbohydrate Choices = 4	1 cup Sambar	2
	½ cup Cabbage Poriyal	0
	1 Roti 6" or 1 plain Dosa	1
	1/3 cup Cooked White/Brown Rice	1
	½ cup Vellarika Pachadi (Cucumber)	0
Afternoon Snack Number of Carbohydrate Choices = 2	1 cup Chai (2% milk)	0
	4 tbsp Fruit/Nut mix	2
Dinner Number of Carbohydrate Choices = 4	1 cup Chicken Chettinad Curry	1
	1/2 cup Rasam	0
	2/3 cup Plain Low-fat Yogurt	1
	2/3 cup cooked White/Brown rice	2

Evening Snack Number of Carbohydrate Choices = 2	1 cup Watermelon Cubes 6 Almonds or Cashews or mix	1 1
Daily Total Number of Carbohydrate Choices		**16**

1800 Calories Sample Menu Plan: North Indian Vegetarian

Daily Calories = 1810 kcal

- Carbohydrates 195 g = 780 kcal (52% of total Calories) = 16 Total Number of Carbohydrate Choices
- Protein 90 g = 360 kcal (24% of total Calories)
- Fat 40 g = 360 kcal (24% of total Calories)

Meal/Snack	Menu: Food and Serving Size	Number of Carbohydrate Choices
Breakfast Number of Carbohydrate Choices = 3	1 6″ diameter Paneer Paratha	2
	2/3 cup Low-Fat Yogurt	1
	1 Cup Chai (2% Milk)	0
Morning Snack Number of Carbohydrate Choices = 1	1 ½ - 2 tbsp Fruit/Nut Mix	1
Lunch Number of Carbohydrate Choices = 4	1.5 cup Vegetable Tofu Stir Fry	1
	2/3 cup White/Brown rice cooked	2
	½ cup Pea Soup	1
Afternoon Snack Number of Carbohydrate Choices = 2	1 cup chopped Raw fruit	1
	6 Almonds or Cashews or mix	1
Dinner Number of Carbohydrate Choices = 4	½ cup Khichadi	1
	2 Roti, 6″ each	2
	½ cup Kadhi	1
	½ cup Okra (Bhindi) Masala	0
Evening Snack Number of Carbohydrate Choices = 2	1 cup 2% Milk	1
	6 Saltine-type crackers	1
	1 tbsp Almond butter	0
Daily Total Number of Carbohydrate Choices		16

1800 Calories Sample Menu Plan: South Indian Vegetarian

Daily Calories = 1773 kcal

- 240g Carbohydrates = 960 kcal (54% of total Calories) = 16 Total Number of Carbohydrate Choices
- 92g Protein = 368 kcal (21% of total Calories)
- 49g Fat = 445 kcal (25% of total Calories)

Meal/Snack	Menu: Food and Serving Size	Number of Carbohydrate Choices
Breakfast Number of Carbohydrate Choices = 3	2 Small Idli	2
	1 tbsp tomato Chutney	0
	1 cup chopped fruit or 1 small fruit	1
Morning Snack Number of Carbohydrate Choices = 1	1 cup Chai (2% milk)	0
	1/3 cup Banana Chips	1
Lunch Number of Carbohydrate Choices = 4	1 cup Sambar	2
	½ cup Cabbage Poriyal	0
	1/3 cup White/Brown Rice cooked	1
	1 Roti, 6"	1
	½ cup Vegetable Pachadi	0
Afternoon Snack Number of Carbohydrate Choices = 2	1 ½-2 tbsp Dry Berries (Trail mix)	1
	2/3 Cup Low-Fat Yogurt	1
Dinner Number of Carbohydrate Choices = 4	2/3 cup Bisi Bhela Bath	2
	½ cup Cucumber Raita	0
	1 Roti, 6"	1
	½ cup Aviyal or Mixed Vegetables Cooked	1
Evening Snack Number of Carbohydrate Choices = 2	6 Almonds or Cashews Mix	1
	1 cup 2% Milk	1
Daily Total Number of Carbohydrate Choices		**16**

2000 Calories Sample Menu Plan: North Indian Non-Vegetarian

Daily Calories = 2020 kcal

- 255 g Carbohydrate = 1020 kcal (50% of total Calories) = 17 Total Number of Carbohydrate Choices
- 118 g Protein = 472 kcal (24% of total Calories)
- 59 g Fat = 528 kcal (26% of total Calories)

Meal/Snack	Menu: Food and Serving Size	Number of Carbohydrate Choices
Breakfast Number of Carbohydrate Choices = 3	2 large Egg Omelet	0
	2 Slices Whole Grain Toast	2
	2 tsp Butter	0
	1 small Fruit (Peach or Pear)	1
	1 cup Chai (2% milk)	0
Morning Snack Number of Carbohydrate Choices = 1	1 oz Veggie sticks (38 Straws)	1
Lunch Number of Carbohydrate Choices = 5	½ cup Toor dal cooked	1
	½ Cup Aloo Gobi	1
	2 Rotis, 6" each	2
	½ cup Sprouted Moong Salad	1
Afternoon Snack Number of Carbohydrate Choices = 2	6 Almonds or Cashews or mix	1
	1 cup chopped Raw Fruit	1
Dinner Number of Carbohydrate Choices = 4	1 cup Chicken Curry	1
	2 Rotis, 6" each	2
	1/3 cup cooked Brown/White Rice	1
	½ cup Cucumber Raita	0
Evening Snack Number of Carbohydrate Choices = 2	1 cup skim milk	1
	3 cup plain popcorn popped	1
	1 tbsp Almond butter	0
Daily Total Number of Carbohydrate Choices		17

2000 Calories Sample Menu Plan: South Indian Non-Vegetarian

Daily Calories = 2008 kcal

- 255 g Carbohydrate = 1020 kcal (50% of total Calories) = 17 Total Number of Carbohydrate Choices
- 118 g Protein = 472 kcal (24% of total Calories)
- 59 g Fat = 528 kcal (26% of total Calories)

Meal/Snack	Menu: Food and Serving Size	Number of Carbohydrate Choices
Breakfast Number of Carbohydrate Choices = 3	2 large Anda (Egg) Bhurji	0
	2 Slices Whole Grain Toast	2
	2 tsp Butter	0
	1 small Fruit (Peach or Pear)	1
	1 cup Chai (2% Milk)	0
Morning Snack Number of Carbohydrate Choices = 1	3 Graham Crackers	1
	1 oz Peanut/Almond Butter	0
Lunch Number of Carbohydrate Choices = 5	1 cup sambar	2
	1 cup Cabbage Poriyal	1
	1 Roti 6"	1
	1/3 cup cooked White/Brown Rice	1
Afternoon Snack Number of Carbohydrate Choices = 2	1 cup Lentil Soup	2
Dinner Number of Carbohydrate Choices = 4	1 cup Chicken Chettinad Curry	1
	½ Cup Rasam	0
	2/3 cup Low-fat Yogurt	1
	⅔ cup cooked White/Brown Rice	2
Evening Snack Number of Carbohydrate Choices = 2	1 small 4" Veggie Uttapam	1
	1 Tbsp Tomato Chutney	0
	1 cup 2% milk	1
Daily Total Number of Carbohydrate Choices		17

2000 Calories Sample Menu Plan: North Indian Vegetarian

Daily Calories = 2016 kcal

- 255 g Carbohydrate = 1020 Kcal (50% of total Calories) = 17 Total Number of Carbohydrate Choices
- 99 g Protein = 396 Kcal (20% of total Calories)
- 67 g Fat = 600 Kcal (30% of total Calories)

Meal/Snack	Menu: Food and Serving Size	Number of Carbohydrate Choices
Breakfast Number of Carbohydrate Choices = 3	1 6″ diameter Paneer Paratha	2
	½ cup Cucumber Raita	0
	1 small Fruit (Peach or Pear)	1
	1 Cup Chai (2% milk)	0
Morning Snack Number of Carbohydrate Choices = 1	1oz (38 Straws) Veggie sticks	1
Lunch Number of Carbohydrate Choices = 5	½ cup Toor dal cooked	1
	1 ½ cup Vegetable Tofu Stir Fry	1
	2/3 cup White/Brown rice cooked	2
	1 Roti 6″	1
Afternoon Snack Number of Carbohydrate Choices = 2	½ cup Sprouted Moong Salad	1
	6 Almonds or Cashews or mix	1
Dinner Number of Carbohydrate Choices = 4	½ cup Vegetable Pulao	1
	1 Roti 6″	1
	1 cup Kadhi	2
	1 cup Okra (Bhindi) Masala	0
Evening Snack Number of Carbohydrate Choices = 2	1 cup Skim milk	1
	6 saltine-type crackers	1
	1 tbsp Almond butter	0
Daily Total Number of Carbohydrate Choices		17

2000 Calories Sample Menu Plan: South Indian Vegetarian

Daily Calories = 2006 kcal

- 255g Carbohydrates = 1020 kcal (51% of total Calories) = 17 Total Number of Carbohydrate Choices
- 98 g Protein = 392 kcal (20% of total Calories)
- 66g Fat = 594 kcal (29% of total Calories)

Meal/Snack	Menu: Food and Serving Size	Number of Carbohydrate Choices
Breakfast Number of Carbohydrate Choices = 3	2 Small Idlis, 3" rounds	2
	½ cup Sambhar	1
	1 tbsp Tomato Chutney	0
	1 Cup Chai (2% milk)	0
Morning Snack Number of Carbohydrate Choices = 1	1/3 Cup Banana Chips	1
Lunch Number of Carbohydrate Choices = 5	1/2 cup Masoor Dal	1
	½ cup Aviyal	1
	2/3 cup White/Brown Rice cooked	2
	1 Appam 8" diameter	1
Afternoon Snack Number of Carbohydrate Choices = 2	6-8 Dry Roasted Mixed Nuts	1
	2/3 Cup Low-fat Fruit Yogurt	1
Dinner Number of Carbohydrate Choices = 4	2/3 Cup Bisi Bhela Bath	2
	1 Roti 6"	1
	½ cup Vegetable Korma	1
Evening Snack Number of Carbohydrate Choices = 2	1cup 2% Milk	1
	1 Small 4" Vegetable Uttapam	1
	1 tbsp Coconut Chutney	0
Daily Total Number of Carbohydrate Choices		17

Carbohydrate Counting Resources

Carbohydrate counting: The basics. (2005). *Clinical Diabetes, 23*(3) 123-124. doi: 10.2337/diaclin.23.3.123

Garduno-Diaz, S.D., & Khokhar, S. (2012). Prevalence, risk factors and complications associated with type 2 diabetes in migrant South Asians. *Diabetes/Metabolism Research and Reviews, 28, 6-24.*

Gopalan, C., Rama Shastri, B. V., & Balasubramanian, S.C. (1989). *Nutritive value of Indian foods.* National Institute of Nutrition, Indian Council of Medical Research.

Gujral, U. P., & Kanaya, A. M. (2021). Epidemiology of diabetes among South Asians in the United States: lessons from the MASALA study. *Annals of the New York Academy of Sciences, 1495(1),* 24–39. https://doi.org/10.1111/nyas.14530

Gujral, U. P., Pradeepa, R., Weber, M. B., Narayan, K. V. & Mohan, V. (2013). Type 2 diabetes in South Asians: similarities and differences with white Caucasian and other populations. *Annals of the New York Academy of Sciences, 1281,* 51-63. doi:10.1111/j.1749-6632.2012.06838.

Holzmeister, L.A. (2010). *The diabetes carbohydrate and fat gram guide.* Academy of Nutrition and Dietetics (AND). Retrieved from www.eatright.org.

Kennedy, M.N. (2014). *Exchange list for meal planning.* Diabetes Teaching Center, University of California, San Francisco.

Kulkarni, K. (2004). Food, culture, and diabetes in the United States. *Clinical Diabetes, 22(4),* 190-192. https://doi.org/10.2337/diaclin.22.4.190

Lee, J.W.R., Brancati, F.L., & Yeh, H.C. (2011). Trends in the Prevalence of Type 2 Diabetes in Asians Versus Whites: Results from the United States National Health Interview Survey, 1997–2008. *Diabetes Care, 34*(2), 353–357. http://doi.org/10.2337/dc100746

Meade, L. T., & Rushton, W. E. (2016). Accuracy of Carbohydrate Counting in Adults. *Clinical Diabetes : A Publication of the American Diabetes Association, 34*(3), 142–147. http://doi.org/10.2337/diaclin.34.3.142

Mohan, V. (2004). Why are Indians more prone to diabetes? *Journal of the Association of Physicians of India, 52,* 468–474.

Muilwijk, M., Nicolaou, M., Qureshi, S. A., Celis-Morales, C., Gill, J. M. R., Sheikh, A., et al. (2018). Dietary and physical activity recommendations to prevent type 2 diabetes in South Asian adults: A systematic review. *PLoS ONE, 13*(7), e0200681. http://doi.org/10.1371/journal.pone.0200681

Nutrition Data System for Research (NDSR). (2017). Nutrition Coordinating Center (NCC), University of Minnesota, Minneapolis, MN. http://www.ncc.umn.edu/services-2/

Rodibaugh, R. *The exchange list system for diabetic meal planning.* University of Arkansas Cooperative Extension Service Printing Services.

Shah, M., Vasandani, C., Adams-Huet, B., & Garg, A. (2018). Comparison of nutrient intakes in South Asians with type 2 diabetesmellitus and controls living in the United States. *Diabetes Research and Clinical Practice, 138,* 47-56. https://doi.org/10.1016/j.diabres.2018.01.016

Unnikrishnan, R., Anjana, R. M., & Mohan, V. (2016). Diabetes mellitus and its complications in India. *Nature reviews. Endocrinology, 12(6),* 357–370. https://doi.org/10.1038/nrendo.2016.53

Warsaw, H.S. & Kulkarni, K. (2011). *ADA complete guide to carbohydrate counting.*
Retrieved from http://www.diabetes.org/food-and-fitness/food/what-can-i- eat/understanding-Carbohydrate/carbohydrate-counting.html

Whiting, D.R., Guariguata, L., Weil, C., & Shaw, J. (2011). IDF diabetes atlas: global estimates of the prevalence of diabetes for 2011 and 2030. *Diabetes Research Clinical Practice, 94,* 311–321.

www.ingramcontent.com/pod-product-compliance
Ingram Content Group UK Ltd.
Pitfield, Milton Keynes, MK11 3LW, UK
UKHW062301290726
14090UKWH00017B/825